Praise for *Creative Cookie Decorating for Everyone*

"Not only is Emily a ray of sunshine and happiness, she is amazingly talented! Her recipes are DELICIOUS and stunningly beautiful with complete instruction for perfect results in anyone's kitchen. This book needs to be in everyone's cookbook collection!"

—Brian Hart Hoffman, editor-in-chief of *Bake from Scratch*

"Emily's cookies are artful, colorful, and fun for the whole family. Now, with this book you too can be a cookie champion."

—Candace Nelson, *Sugar Rush* judge and founder of Sprinkles and Pizzana

"I marvel at how Emily decorates cookies! It is truly an art form that she is teaching. I love the beautiful step by step photos for every cookie and the easy technique she shares. For me she takes the fear out of cookie decorating with this book."

—Gemma Stafford, Bigger Bolder Baking

"Emily Hutchinson's *Creative Cookie Decorating For Everyone* is the ultimate handbook for creating the most gorgeous cookies ever. With detailed step-by-step instructions and incredible process shots galore, Emily has created the most approachable yet stunning designs that can totally be mastered by beginners. Your guests will be completely wowed!"

—Jocelyn Delk Adams, award-winning author of
Grandbaby Cakes: Modern Recipes, Vintage Charm, Soulful Memories

"Emily has mastered balancing baking techniques with stellar taste, making edible cookie art that's easy, approachable, and inventive for all dessert lovers. Her ability to teach precise skills through thoughtful instructions and step-by-step photographs makes this an essential cookbook for bakers of all skill levels."

—Kelly Senyei, founder of Just a Taste and author of *The Secret Ingredient Cookbook*

Praise for Emily Hutchinson & *Creative Cookie Decorating*

"She is a cookie goddess!"

—**Rachael Ray**

"Talk about gorgeous. This is a gorgeous book."

—**Lance Bass**

"I've never seen someone decorate a cookie better, and I've never tasted better cookies. . . . [t]he best buttercream icing I've ever had."

—**Debbie Matenopoulos, cohost of Hallmark Channel's** *Home & Family* **and author of** *It's All Greek to Me*

"Emily is talented and has a very clean and beautiful aesthetic to her work. . . . She offers a modern twist to traditional recipes."

—**Sugey Palomares,** *Family Circle* **magazine**

"Love love love these cookies! Tutorials are easy to follow, yet make expert-looking buttercream designs. The honey marble glaze is my favorite. Delicious and gorgeous! Emily takes sugar cookies to a whole new fabulous level!"

—**Stephen Lowry of SHOWBOY Bakeshop, Food Network's Cake Wars champion**

"This is a must-have for anyone in love with the art of decorated cookies. Her tutorials and recipes are an indispensable resource for anyone interested in learning to decorate cookies with buttercream icing. In addition to the treasure trove of information, Emily's inspiring story about how her personal journey led her to cookie decorating will touch your heart."

—**Callye Alvarado, founder of Sweet Sugar Belle, product designer/cookie decorator**

"Emily makes buttercream cookie designs accessible to anyone willing to learn! Her tutorials are not only aplenty (with a huge variety), but also come with clear instructions. Beginners and seasoned buttercream decorators alike will have so much fun going through all the different projects to learn and to receive inspiration to create their own designs."

—**Lisa He of Borderlands Bakery, Food Network** *Christmas Cookie Challenge* **champion, and as seen on Netflix's** *Sugar Rush*

"Tastes phenomenal, incredible . . . so beautiful."

—**Lacey Chabert, American actress as seen in** *Mean Girls*

Creative Cookie Decorating

FOR EVERYONE

BUTTERCREAM FROSTING RECIPES, DESIGNS,
AND TIPS FOR EVERY OCCASION

Emily Hutchinson

Photography by Johanna Martinson, Johannah Chadwick, and Emily Hutchinson

New York, New York

Good Books books may be purchased in bulk at special discounts for sales promotion, corporate gifts, fund-raising, or educational purposes. Special editions can also be created to specifications. For details, contact the Special Sales Department, Good Books, 307 West 36th Street, 11th Floor, New York, NY 10018 or info@skyhorsepublishing.com.

Good Books is an imprint of Skyhorse Publishing, Inc.®, a Delaware corporation.

Visit our website at www.goodbooks.com.

10 9 8 7 6 5 4 3 2 1

Library of Congress Cataloging-in-Publication Data is available on file.

Cover design by Daniel Brount
Cover photograph by Johannah Chadwick

Special thanks for:
Photography:
   How-to photos / Johanna Martinson
   Kitchen how-to photos, cover photo, author photos, family photos / Johannah Chadwick
   Cookie plate photos for each cookie design, recipe photos / Emily Hutchinson
   Cookie cutters: Brighton cutters, Inspired to taste, Emma's Sweets, The cookie cutter shop, HolFox cutters
Vanilla beans: Trafton and Sons
Navy polka dot dress and navy floral dress: Draper James

Print ISBN: 978-1-68099-719-4
Ebook ISBN: 978-1-68099-720-0

Printed in China

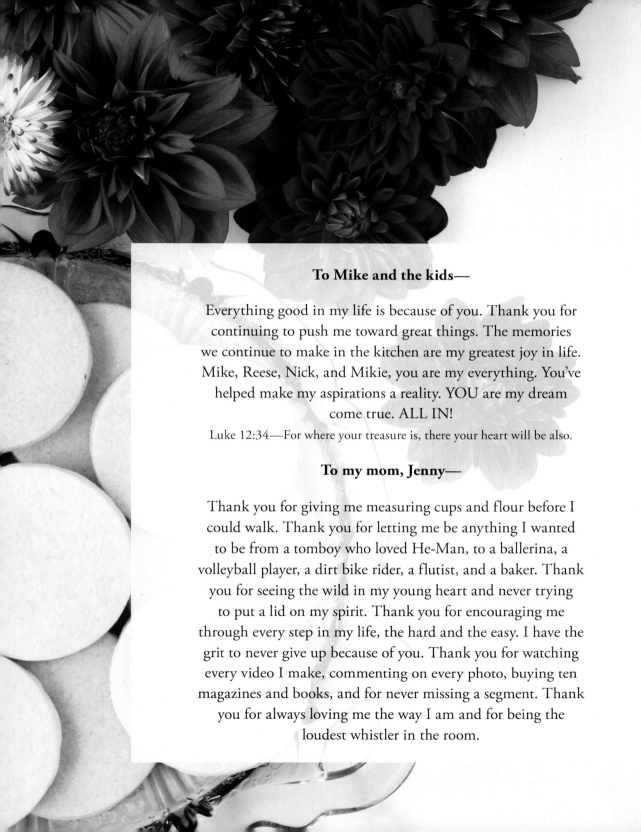

To Mike and the kids—

Everything good in my life is because of you. Thank you for
continuing to push me toward great things. The memories
we continue to make in the kitchen are my greatest joy in life.
Mike, Reese, Nick, and Mikie, you are my everything. You've
helped make my aspirations a reality. YOU are my dream
come true. ALL IN!

Luke 12:34—For where your treasure is, there your heart will be also.

To my mom, Jenny—

Thank you for giving me measuring cups and flour before I
could walk. Thank you for letting me be anything I wanted
to be from a tomboy who loved He-Man, to a ballerina, a
volleyball player, a dirt bike rider, a flutist, and a baker. Thank
you for seeing the wild in my young heart and never trying
to put a lid on my spirit. Thank you for encouraging me
through every step in my life, the hard and the easy. I have the
grit to never give up because of you. Thank you for watching
every video I make, commenting on every photo, buying ten
magazines and books, and for never missing a segment. Thank
you for always loving me the way I am and for being the
loudest whistler in the room.

Contents

Introduction

The opportunity to write a second book was exciting, and to be able to teach in another book had only been part of my wildest dreams. If you have the first book, you know my story. If you don't, let me give you this condensed version of how I started baking:

When I was a little girl, my mom had me playing with measuring spoons, cups, flour, and sugar from the time I could walk. We baked boxed cupcakes and chocolate chip cookies together. I was always fascinated with being in the kitchen. My grandma really taught me to bake when I was around five years old—by *baking*, I mean we were baking breads and pies together. I remember my first pumpkin bread; I was so proud because it was delicious, and I was finally baking something that tasted good. They were a step up from my flour dough pieces drenched in cinnamon sugar. Baking together was our special bonding time; we did this together for years until she sadly lost her battle with cancer. Baking wasn't the same after she died.

I still baked and had a talent and passion for it, but it was more of a holiday thing than a weekly baking obsession. Fast forward to having two amazing children, Reese and Nick, and to meeting my husband, Mike, who became their stepdad. Mike and I decided to have a child of our own in 2007 and named her Jennifer. We called her Jenny or Jenny Lou. She was the missing piece to our blended family. When Jenny was two and a half months old, she suddenly passed away in her sleep; it was classified as SIDS because they couldn't find a reason for her death. This left us broken, angry, and beyond devastated.

Time seemed to go on, but I was stuck. Stuck in my grief and sadness. The pain from losing her just wouldn't subside. I was sinking deeper into a pit of despair. Losing a child feels like your heart is physically broken and you can't fully breathe in. We were all trying to survive this devastation together. The trauma of that day lives in the forefront of my mind like it was yesterday.

Luke 1:45 "Blessed is she who has believed that the Lord would fulfil his promises to her."

Friends of ours noticed our struggle and invited us to church, and we were saved that day. Our lives changed. I began to breathe again, smile, and find joy. I decided to get back to my baking roots and shook off those old measuring cups. Everything flooded back to me and a fire in my soul ignited. For the first time since we lost our Jenny, I had found hope and peace, and I had found it in my kitchen. I created original buttercream frosted cookie tutorials on Instagram that went viral. I could feel my journey starting.

I have since worked very hard and have been beyond blessed with God's opened doors. There is not one thing or one person in my life that I take for granted; I think the unfathomable loss of my daughter has contributed to that. I know what it's like to have a little and have a lot. I am so grateful and thankful that you're here, reading this and becoming part of my journey. My hope for you is that you're now on a sweet journey of your own. I love sharing our story, and I know it's not baking-related, but it's my story. I think there is value in sharing and connecting in our weakness and also celebrating triumphs. I think, to understand me, my heart, and why I am so passionate about what I do, you have to know what makes me, me.

About Me

I am not professionally trained; however, I think some of the best chefs and bakers are taught at a young age and grow from what they know.

Baking is in my blood; my grandma was an incredible baker, and my aunt is, too. I grew up coveting family recipes and never share them. I do, however, enjoy sharing my own recipes. I fell in love at the early age of five, but really started baking seriously in 2010 and started documenting my bakes in 2013. I always tell people to keep practicing because it's taken me years of hard work, tears, and prayers to get here.

I've worked with the Hallmark Channel; I was a cookie-decorator and friend of the *Home and Family Show* before it ended in 2021. I landed one of two seats as a judge on Hallmark Drama's *Christmas Cookie Matchup*. I also do segments with *The Rachael Ray Show* and live television, as well. I have traveled all over the United States teaching my tips and tricks to help people learn. I've taught celebrities like Lance Bass from NSYNC and Candace Nelson, the Sprinkles cupcakes founder and *Sugar Rush* judge. I've partnered with Williams Sonoma to teach online courses. I have been featured in *Southern Living* and other online articles, but one of my proudest achievements was being featured in *Bake from Scratch's Holiday COOKIES Collector's Edition*— my work was on the cover as well as inside the magazine as a sixteen-page spread.

I am a small-town girl, a mother, and a wife. I live in the same town where my parents and grandparents went to school. The same high school English teacher who taught my sisters also taught my daughter. I am content and happy to see my family raised as I was.

I would love to go back to school someday to add to my pastry skills, but until then, I will keep making messes in my kitchen while trying to find the perfect formulas to share with you. My mom and I have joked about me looking like a mad scientist as I run around my kitchen yelling, "IT WORKED!!! IT WORKED!!!!" Lots of successes and lots of failures. I throw away more dough from experimenting than I like to admit, but that's all part of the growing process.

While shooting photos for this book with my sister, I was nearly in tears because I had finally created a cookie I had been working on for a while, but when the cookies cooled off, they were no longer soft pillows—they were dry. I was sharing the obstacles I'd run into and how many times I had to test one recipe to get it right, when she looked at me and said, "Em, this is why it's YOU. This is why you do what you do."

And she's right. It's very important that the recipes you've grown to love and trust from my first book, *Creative Cookie Decorating*, can also be trusted in this new book. I take pride in helping others hone their baking and decorating skills. I hope you find some inspiration within these pages and become passionate about decorating with me.

If there's one thing I know, it's cookies!

You can!

It's important to know that my first cookies all those years ago were not as pretty as you might think. Practice and diligence make perfection. Give yourself a handful of times to practice before you throw in the piping bag. Show yourself grace and keep going. You might have a talent you didn't even know was there.

I hope this book gives you gumption to start your own page, business, or even just feel a little more comfortable contributing to holidays and birthdays. The best thing in life is to live sweetly and be unapologetically you. Put your personal touch on cookie designs, add in color and flare to make it your own. You can do this!!!! Follow what's in your heart. Surround yourself with people who cheer loudly for you. The baking community online is very helpful and supportive. You will learn the most from just doing, so make today the day you start!!

Let's get familiar

To ensure successful cookies, read through the recipe and instructions in their entirety before you start baking. Make certain you are prepped and ready with all ingredients to prevent having to run to the store. It helps to plan out what you need in advance. I want you to get familiar with decorating and flooding with buttercream.

Jeremiah 29:11
"For I know the plans I have for you," declares the Lord,
"Plans to prosper you and not to harm you, plans to give you hope and a future."

The techniques I'm sharing with you work best for me. My hope is that I can prevent you from the fails I've had along the way. My recipes have evolved over the years, as has my baking. I think the way for us to learn and grow is from failures and mistakes.

I use circles, squares, and rectangles in many different ways. I absolutely adore a cute cookie cutter but not everyone has access to those. In those cases, you can find templates online to print, cut, and make your own cookie shapes.

I have added Master Tips at the bottom where needed to ensure you have the most helpful information before you start. **Be sure to read those**; they are important tips.

How to Use This Book

Things to know

Included in each recipe are things you need **From the kitchen** and **From the drawer.** (If you have *Creative Cookie Decorating*, you'll recognize this setup!)

From the kitchen are the cookies and buttercream you will need (recipes for those are featured earlier in the book). I also listed items such as hot water or a microwave, which are normal kitchen staples. From the drawer are items like tips, piping bags, spatulas, food colorings, sprinkles, and all the goodies to decorate that we generally keep in a drawer out of sight.

I recommend you read the full instructions, techniques, ingredients, and Master Tips before you start on a cookie set. I try to clean as I go, and I always put supplies back in their spot for next time. Do not substitute; use what is recommended in each recipe. I use Costco Salted Sweet Cream Butter and Crisco vegetable shortening in my signature recipes. Some people frown on using shortening in buttercream, but I find the shortening makes for a creamier, smoother buttercream. If you don't like that, using only butter works.

Don't skip reading this part!

- Check expiration dates; if it's been sitting in the back of the cupboard for months or years, it's bad. Shortening goes rancid if it sits for too long; in a hot climate, the shelf life of shortening is even shorter than expected. It will develop a taste that is terrible and will become oily. Butter, baking powder, and flour also expire.
- Vanilla extract should be pure, because the flavor is essential to delicious cookies.
- Softened butter means taking it out of the refrigerator an hour before baking. The butter should be solid and leave a small indentation when you press your finger into it. Never use a microwave. Mushy butter will cause unwanted spreading of cookies.
- Use a cheese grater to grate cold butter straight into your mixing bowl if you forget to take your butter out of the refrigerator
- If you can find Kirkland or Lucerne brand Salted Sweet Cream Butter, I suggest using that and omitting salt all together, because these brands have the perfect amount of salt for these cookies.

- I ask you to add salt before creaming the butter, so the salt is evenly distributed into your dough and you won't get any salt granules in your bite.
- If the dough seems dry, KEEP MIXING. It will all come together.
- If the recipe says to add more milk to achieve desired consistency of buttercream, add more. (Gah, I wish I could be in your kitchen with you to help!) You'll need less milk in the summer, and more in the winter. To pipe flowers, you'll want stiffer buttercream, and when piping back and forth, you'll want it to be a little softer so it flows better. If you use heavy cream, it's a lot thicker than milk, so you'll need more.
- For my recipes, I use the scoop-and-level method. I use a spoon to scoop in flour or powdered sugar into my cup. The flour should mound over your cup. I do this over a plate or over the bag so there isn't a huge mess. Take the flat back of a butter knife or metal spatula and level off the measuring cup. When I pack my brown sugar, I scoop it in, pack it down with my hands, and make sure its level before adding it. If you have a kitchen scale, it is the most accurate you can get. I have added gram measurements for all ingredients throughout the book to help you. These measurements come from my kitchen; if you Google how many grams in flour, it won't be the same.
- Aluminum-free baking powder should be double acting, which means it's activated in mixing stage and baking stage. It's best to keep aluminum out if we can, so I get aluminum free. Aluminum gives a metallic taste that isn't ideal in a delicately sweet sugar cookie.
- Don't knead the dough. The more you have to re-roll, the tougher the cookies will become if you're adding flour each time.
- Something to be aware of: If you're using a hand mixer, you will have to press dough together once the flour is all mixed in. The hand mixer won't bring the dough into one ball; it will keep cutting it up.
- Refrigeration is very important to solidify the fats before baking. If you don't refrigerate, your cookies can spread.
- When baking your cookies, the more space you give them, the better they hold their shape. The closer together they are, the more they will "steam" and spread. Spread them out two inches. If you have to bake in smaller batches, that's okay.
- Use an offset spatula to reform your cookies right when you pull them out of the oven.
- I am not an expert in gluten-free or dairy-free baking, but I have added recipes or tips that are sensitive to those allergies because I want cookies to be enjoyed by all. I found that Earth Balance Soy Free Buttery Spread in the tub works best for dairy free.

I use Bob's Red Mill 1 to 1 Flour to make cookies gluten free.

- Everyone has a different oven, so please know your oven before you start baking. The cook time for the cookies is crucial to baking that perfect cookie. Bake them until they puff up in the center or to the time noted. It's okay to add on another minute if you're questioning it. I do like a softer and slightly undercooked cookie.

- Temperature, humidity, and elevation can make it so you have to alter accordingly. I have provided a chart in the back of the book to help you (see page 352).

- Coloring buttercream can be difficult for some; I use a variety of brands for my colors. Be sure to use gel food coloring unless instructed otherwise.

- Flooding with buttercream takes longer but makes for a more solid surface resembling royal icing. Follow the instructions and heat times or you will have a runny mess. The buttercream crusts up, so you have to work quickly and then return to heat to resume working.

- We are baking the cookies at 375°F for about 6 to 9 minutes, depending on the recipe. For those that state 350°F for 10 to 11 minutes, it's because we are baking lower and slower to avoid browning too quickly on the bottom of the cookies. If you ever find your cookies are browning too quickly, turn the oven from 375°F to 350°F and bake for 2 to 3 minutes longer, following the "puff up in the center rule" in my recipe instructions.

- I find that parchment paper will make the cookie brown quicker, and a restaurant-grade aluminum cookie sheet with no parchment paper bakes cookies perfectly with no browning on the bottom. I suggest investing in a couple restaurant-grade aluminum cookie sheets to avoid browning on bottoms.

- Freeze bare, unfrosted cookies for a couple hours/overnight. I prefer to freeze the cookies overnight because it gives them added moisture to keep them soft. Pull cookies out of freezer 1 hour before frosting them.

- The cornstarch will help keep nice crisp edges; I recommend using it. Add in a couple teaspoons to any recipe listed in this book.

- Nice and thick cookies balance out the sweetness of the buttercream, so don't make them thinner than ¼ inch.

- Frosted cookies can be frozen for a week or two before an event. If you want to freeze them, be gentle and treat them like frosted cupcakes. When you pull them out of the freezer, be sure to allow the buttercream to crust back over.

- Always store in an airtight container to preserve freshness and keep the cookies soft.

- Cookies can be bagged after 24 hours; the flooding buttercream holds a nice crust and is more solid than regular crusting buttercream.
- If you cream your butter and sugars too much, it can lead to slight cracks in the baked cookie, so cream as instructed.

- A way to spread love and sweetness during the holidays is making up cookie boxes to bring to neighbors, first responders, and nursing homes. Bring your kids with you to deliver; teach them to serve and give to people when nothing is expected in return. I've never seen an unhappy person who has been gifted with a box of cookies—it's just not possible. Cookies make everyone happy. Bake someone's day!

Essentials

Cheese grater:
Also known as a shredder. Metal kitchen utensil that grates food into small pieces.

Cookie scribe:
A small tool with a pointed edge to help etch in a cookie or to work frosting into small corners. A toothpick will work in place of a scribe.

Cookie sheet:
An evenly heating, rustproof aluminum baking sheet without a parchment paper liner works best. Nonstick with parchment works but cookie bottoms will brown faster.

Cookie spatula:
A thin, flat stainless-steel tool used to lift cookies off a baking sheet.

Food coloring gel:
A concentrated edible dye that minimizes the amount of liquid needed to color frosting.

Food Processor:
Kitchen appliance with a sharp blade that is used to blend food without liquid.

Measuring cups and spoons:
Cups and spoons marked with amounts used for baking.

Microplane:
For zesting citrus. Large handle with long, skinny zesting blade made from stainless steel to get thin, fluffy shreds of zest.

Mixing bowl:
A deep bowl that can mix ingredients together or, in this case, mix buttercream colors and flavors in small batches.

Offset or angled spatula:
Flat and thin with a handle used for spreading and smoothing. It is angled to keep your fingers off the icing. Use a 4-inch or 6-inch spatula.

Plastic coupler:
This is a plastic part that connects your tip to your piping bag and allows that tip to be changed easily.

Piping or pastry bag:
Hand-held bag made from cloth or plastic that holds the buttercream while decorating. I prefer the plastic bags.

Rubber spatula:
An essential kitchen tool for gently scraping or stirring mixtures.

Sifter:
Used to break up or separate clumps in the dry ingredients. You can also use a wire mesh strainer to sift.

Squeeze bottle:
A type of plastic container with tip attached that allows liquid to flow out.

Springform pan:
A round cake pan that has a removable bottom and sides that open up and close with a clasp.

Stand Mixer:
A large mixer that has a bowl that locks into place as it's mixing. They have many attachments; I use the paddle attachment throughout this book. It can operate on its own with various speeds for mixing.

Tipless piping bags:
A piping bag that allows you to simply cut the tip off and start piping; great for flooding with buttercream.

Tips:
Small metal or plastic nozzles attached to the end of the piping bag that is an essential part of decorating. The sizes vary. The large tips do not require couplers.

Wire cooling rack:
This will allow air to circulate through cookies to help the cooling process. Use a tight grid cooling rack for cookies.

Wire whisk:
Used to blend ingredients.

Techniques

Filling Your Piping Bag

I've included even the simplest tasks with photos and instructions to help!

From the kitchen	**From the drawer**
Batch of buttercream	Piping bags
	Coupler
	Tip
	Scissors
	Clear plastic wrap
	optional (see Two-Toned
	Buttercream instructions,
	page 26)

Instructions

1. Cut your piping bag about 1 inch up from the tip.
2. Drop your coupler inside the bag.
3. Attach piping tip to plastic coupler on the outside and fill the bag with ½ to 1 cup of buttercream.

MASTER TIP

Don't overfill your buttercream. It warms up quickly in your hand and your flowers will get droopy. It's easier to pipe and guide your hand with less in your bag. Keep refilling for the best results.

Parchment Method

This method is very simple and effective. All you will need is parchment and a spatula, you could also use a butter knife if you don't have an offset spatula.

From the kitchen	**From the drawer**
Batch of buttercream	Tip 10
Cookies	Angled offset spatula
	Parchment paper

Instructions

1. Pipe buttercream on a cookie using tip 10 and let crust for 10 minutes.
2. Use spatula to smooth the surface.
3. Place a small piece of parchment paper over the frosted cookie and gently smooth the surface. Let crust for 15 minutes.
4. Pull away parchment paper to reveal a smooth surface. Place parchment back on and re-smooth if the surface has any imperfections.

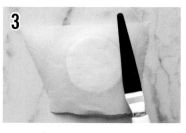

MASTER TIP

Use this on any surface to get a smooth top. It's so simple and effective. Cut a piece of parchment a little bigger than your cookie. Too big of sheet can crumple. Don't let the parchment bunch.

Flooding with Buttercream

I tried experimenting with flooding buttercream about seven years ago. It was undocumented so it's almost like it never happened, but what I learned then helps us now. I loved the smooth look, but it took a few extra steps, which seemed a little overwhelming.

I wanted to introduce this technique because it's such a beautiful look that is very popular; it looks like royal icing but tastes soft and delicious like buttercream. This is technical, and it's not easy. You will make a handful of mistakes in your own kitchen before you get the consistency that's right for you. Each day has been different for me, but I always start out with the same recipe and then add more heavy cream as needed. Temperature outside and the warmth of your kitchen can determine how much cream you'll need. Heating in very short, small bursts and then stirring is crucial to getting the flood consistency right. I heat in the microwave for 4- to 5- second increments. If you overheat, the butter will melt and separate, and the buttercream will also run right off the cookie. If you don't heat it enough, you won't get a flat, smooth surface. It's tricky, but you can do it.

A few decorators online only use flooding buttercream. I'm always so impressed with the patience and time it takes to do it. This is not for the faint of heart.

I have found that heavy cream makes a thicker and flatter surface with fewer ripples. Milk is better for buttercream you aren't flooding with. Add a little at a time, by the teaspoon.

From the kitchen
Batch of buttercream for flooding
Heavy cream

From the drawer
Food coloring gel
Scribe or toothpick
Squeeze bottle with tip 2 attached or
 tipless piping bags

Instructions

1. In a small bowl, add 1 cup of flooding buttercream. Add in a few drops of desired food coloring and mix. With a spatula, stir until desired color is reached.

2. Pour ½ cup into a tipless piping bag and cover the bowl with the remaining buttercream with plastic wrap. A crust will form. Tie a knot in the end of the piping bag to prevent any air coming in or buttercream drizzling out.

3. Snip a tiny hole at the end of the piping bag and outline the cookie. Quickly fill in with a steady back and forth stream of buttercream. If using a thicker piping consistency around the edge to act as a dam for flooding the buttercream, you will require a separate bag and a little thicker or cooler buttercream so it stands up to the warmer buttercream.

4. Use a scribe or a toothpick to go around the cookie and get out any bumps. Use short swirling motions all the way around.

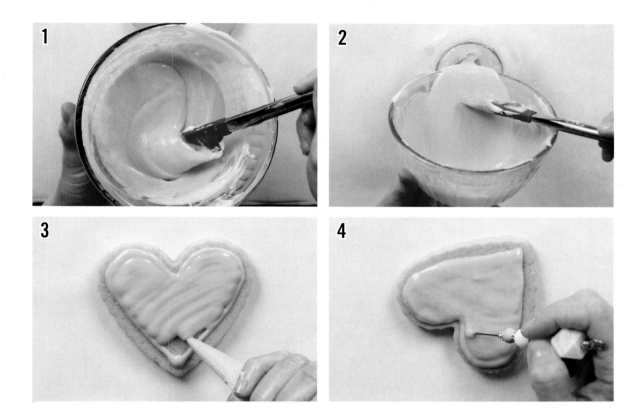

MASTER TIP

This technique is challenging. You must also work in stages because the buttercream cools quickly. You can keep a warmer or a heating pad nearby to make sure the buttercream doesn't cool between piping. If using a squeeze bottle, a crust will start to form on top of the flood-consistency buttercream the more you reheat it. If storing the buttercream, make sure it's in an airtight container.

Dip Method

I love this dip method because it's so simple and easy enough for anyone to do. My kids love this method because they feel very accomplished with just a dip of the cookie. Dazzle them up with sprinkles or let them dry and pipe buttercream on top.

From the kitchen
Flood-consistency buttercream (see page 126)

From the drawer
Bowl
Food coloring gel
Knife or toothpick
Cooling rack
Parchment paper

Instructions

1. Fill a bowl with 1 to 2 cups of flood-consistency buttercream, and add in three drops of gel food coloring.

2. Take a knife, skewer, or toothpick and make swirls on the surface. Don't mix. The swirls add a marbled color. You can do one solid color if your intention isn't to marble the cookie.

3. Take a cookie and dip it straight into the swirled buttercream, pull straight up, and let the excess drip off.

4. Turn over to reveal the beautiful marbled buttercream and a giant smile. Place on a cooling rack with parchment paper under it to catch any drippings and let dry.

MASTER TIP

The buttercream will form a thin crust if left uncovered. Add in drops as you go; add three drops food coloring to start, and halfway through, add another and give it another swirl. Liquid food coloring will also work in this recipe. Add sprinkles for some zhoosh.

Two-Toned Buttercream

Two-toning buttercream with food coloring leaves a delicate line of color through the butter-cream. This technique turns flower petal tips colors or makes the center of a petal a different color. Prepare to be changed by the plastic wrap trick you're about to see (if you didn't see it in the first book)! I use the plastic wrap trick even when I'm not using two colors because it makes it so easy to just grab out the plastic and throw it away. This method keeps the butter-cream from warming in your hand so quickly. You won't have to dig through buttercream to get your coupler out, and you can reuse the thick plastic piping bags.

From the kitchen	From the drawer
Batch of buttercream	Clear plastic wrap
	Food-safe paint brush
	Red food coloring gel
	Piping bag
	Coupler
	Scissors
	Tip

Instructions

1. Lay a piece of plastic wrap down horizontally. Dip a food-safe paint brush in concentrated gel color. Paint a thin stripe horizontally about 6 inches long.

2. Layer about 1 cup of white buttercream over top of the color stripe. Fold over hot-dog style to create a pouch—a buttercream burrito is what I like to call it. Twist up your ends and coil up one side so the buttercream doesn't come out.

3. Feed the uncoiled end though your coupler. Cut the end of your piping bag about 1 inch from the tip and drop in the end with attached coupler straight down into the piping bag.

4. Pull the plastic through and cut off remaining. Attach tip and match up the strip with the end you want the color to come out of. Begin to pipe. The white buttercream will pull the color through. You will have to give it a big squeeze to see the colors come through. If you want the color to come through in the tips of the petals, have the color line up with the skinny end of the tip. For the inside of the petals, have the color lined up with the wide end of the tip.

5. Begin to pipe, adjusting the tip for color flow.

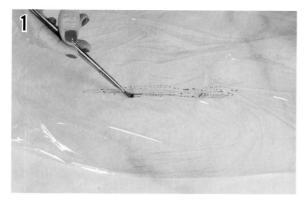

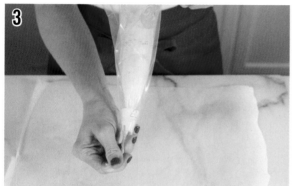

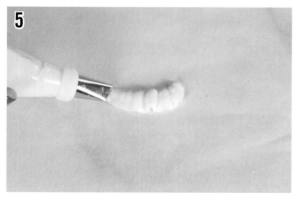

MASTER TIP

As you're piping, you will see where the color is going. You can adjust the 104 tips to make it flow from the wide side or the skinny side. I always give the buttercream a big squeeze before I start to make sure my color is flowing right.

Multi-Colored Buttercream

This technique is so beautiful because it allows a little hint of each color to come through in the buttercream as you're piping.

From the kitchen	From the drawer
Batch of buttercream	Clear plastic wrap
Cookies	Food-safe paint brush
	Red, orange, yellow, blue, green, purple, and pink food coloring gel
	Coupler
	Piping bag
	Tip

Instructions

1. Lay a piece of plastic wrap down horizontally. Dip paint brush in one concentrated gel color. Paint a thin strip horizontally about 6 inches long. Leave a very small space and then repeat with the next gel color. Remember to leave space between each color and continue until you've used the colors of the rainbow.

2. Layer on about a cup of white buttercream over top of the color stripes.

3. Fold over hot-dog style to create a pouch/buttercream burrito. Twist up your ends and coil up one side so the buttercream doesn't come out.

4. Feed the other end though your coupler. Cut the end of your piping bag about 1 inch and drop in the end of your plastic wrap with attached coupler straight down into the piping bag.

5. Pull the plastic through and cut off remainder.

6. Attach tip and match the stripe up with the end you want the color to come out of. Begin to pipe. The white buttercream will pull the colors through. You will have to give it a big squeeze to start to see the colors come through.

MASTER TIP

This multi-colored technique will work on flowers, too, with just one color or two shades of the same color. Explore the possibilities!

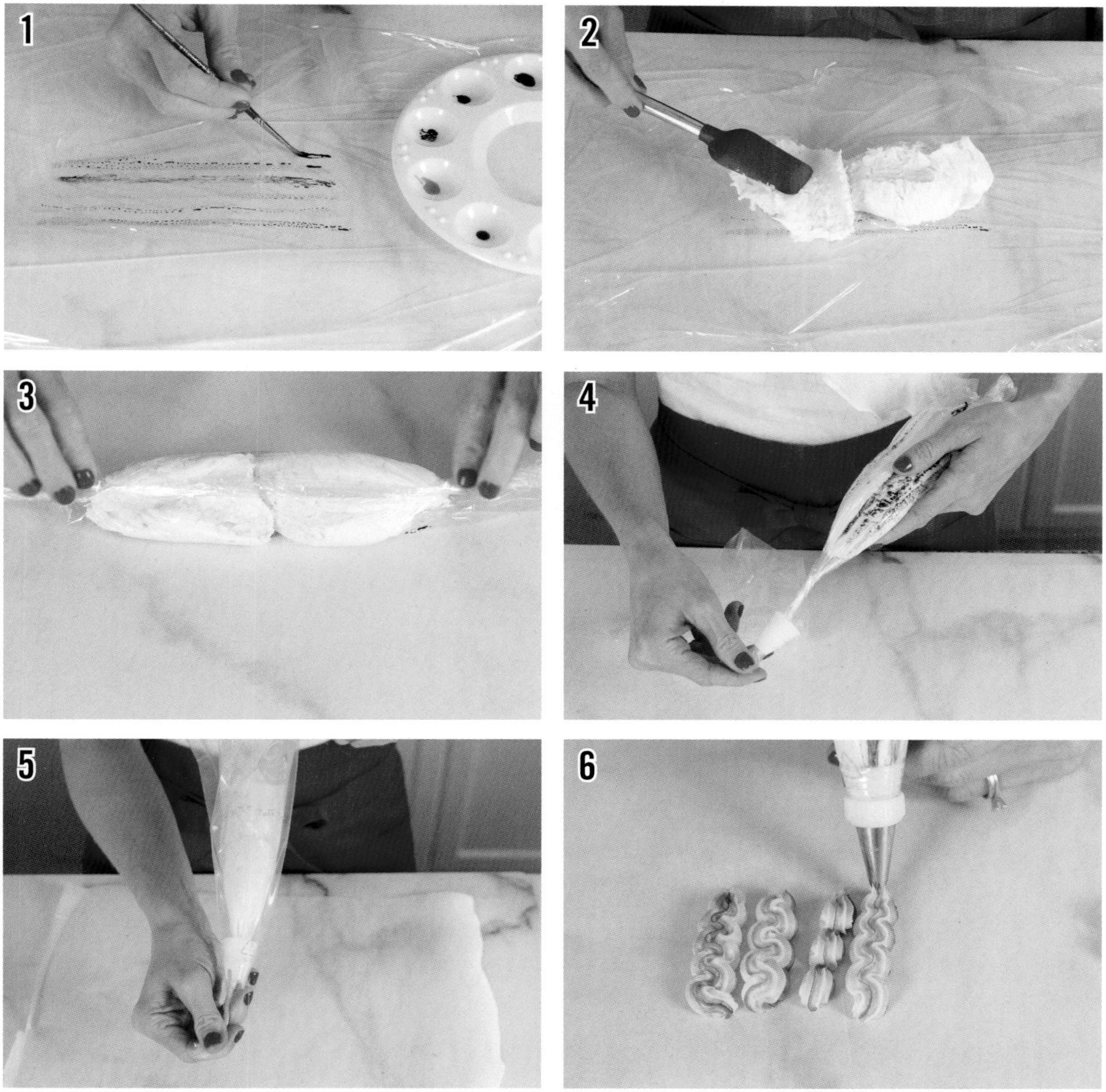
1
2
3
4
5
6

Freezer Frosting Method

This technique makes everyone excited because it's very approachable. I am showing you how to make a solid color or a watercolor look. Add multiple colors for a beautiful surface. My kids are obsessed with this because it's so fun and simple. You can decorate on top of the freezer frosting method, too. So many possibilities!

From the kitchen	From the drawer
Batch of buttercream	Cookie sheet
Cookies	Parchment paper
Cup of hot water	Angled spatula
Bowl of hot water	Cookie cutter
	Offset spatula
	Pink food coloring

Instructions for solid freezer frosting

1. Take a cookie sheet that will fit in your freezer and lay a piece of parchment paper on it to fit. Spread 2 cups of buttercream on the parchment with an angled spatula until it's ¼ to ⅜ inch thick. (You can also do a small amount more for a couple cookies; I am doing a single cookie here.)

2. Dip angled spatula in hot cup of water for 30 seconds or more. When the spatula is warm, pull it out and spread the buttercream. It will melt and become smooth. Repeat until the surface is flat. Freeze for 2 hours or overnight.

Continued on next page

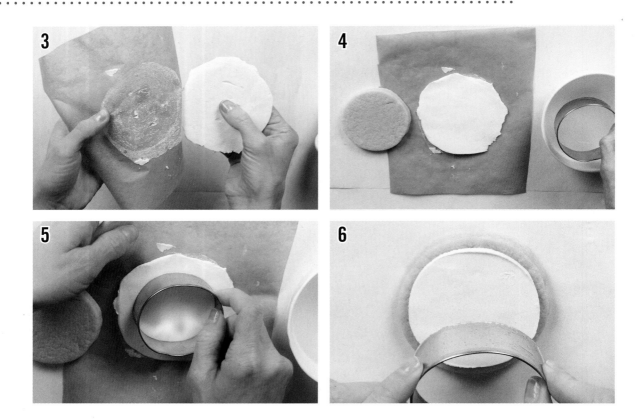

3. After it's frozen, gently and quickly peel parchment away and set the frosting back down on the parchment and frozen cookie sheet to stay cold.

4. Fill a bowl with very hot water. Place a cookie cutter that's the same shape as your cookie into the hot water to warm it up.

5. Firmly press the cookie cutter into the buttercream and quickly move it to your cookie (the buttercream should be inside the cookie cutter). It's an easy transfer unless the buttercream is too soft.

6. Gently push it through onto the cookie and smooth any sides quickly with an offset spatula. A warm spatula works best.

Instructions for watercolor freezer frosting

1. Take a cookie sheet that will fit in your freezer and lay a piece of parchment paper on it to fit. Spread 2 cups of buttercream on the parchment with an angled spatula until it's ¼- to ⅜-inch thick. (You can also do a small amount more for a couple cookies.)

2. Dip angled spatula in hot cup of water for 30 seconds or more. When spatula is warm, pull it out and spread the buttercream. It will melt and become smooth. Repeat until the surface is flat.

3. Take some pink buttercream and pipe dots sporadically on top of the white buttercream.

4. Again, dip spatula into hot water and smooth the color onto the white surface. Make small swirling motions to create a watercolor look. Freeze for 2 hours or overnight. Cut buttercream like instructed above.

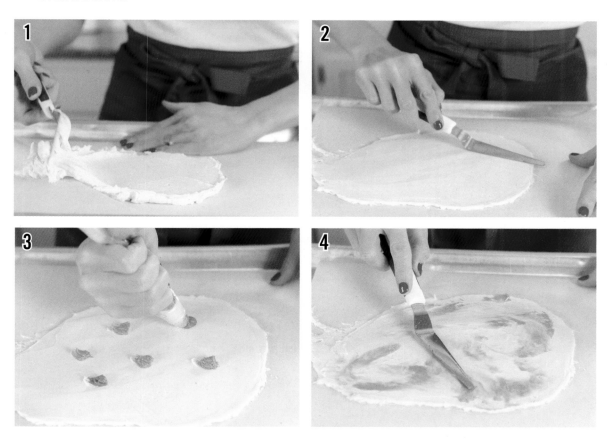

MASTER TIP

The hotter the spatula, the flatter the buttercream will become.

Frozen Flat Technique

From the kitchen
Batch of buttercream
Cookies
Cup hot water

From the drawer
Tip 10
Parchment paper
Angled spatula
Sugar crystals (optional)

Instructions

1. Pipe buttercream on a cookie using tip 10 or larger round tip..

2. Turn cookie over directly onto parchment paper and gently press—don't press too hard or the buttercream will smush out. Freeze for 2 hours or overnight.

3. Dip spatula in hot water. Pull away parchment paper and smooth any imperfections with the angled spatula. Dip in sugar crystals or pipe on design.

MASTER TIP

Use this technique to make a base of a cookie to pipe designs onto or to simply add sprinkles to. Easily do a dozen cookies or more!

Smooth Buttercream Technique

From the kitchen	From the drawer
Batch of buttercream	Angled spatula
Cookies	Tip 5, 10, or 12
1 cup hot water	Kitchen towel

Instructions

1. Pipe on buttercream with tip 12 to cover cookie.

2. Smooth buttercream on your cookie with angled spatula.

3. Dip angled spatula in hot water for 10 seconds and quickly dry.

4. Smooth buttercream with heated spatula until smooth. Repeat if needed.

MASTER TIP

Continue to heat up the water and spatula and smooth the cookie until desired smoothness is achieved. Pipe different colors on the buttercream with a small round tip as you're smoothing to get a marbled look on the buttercream.

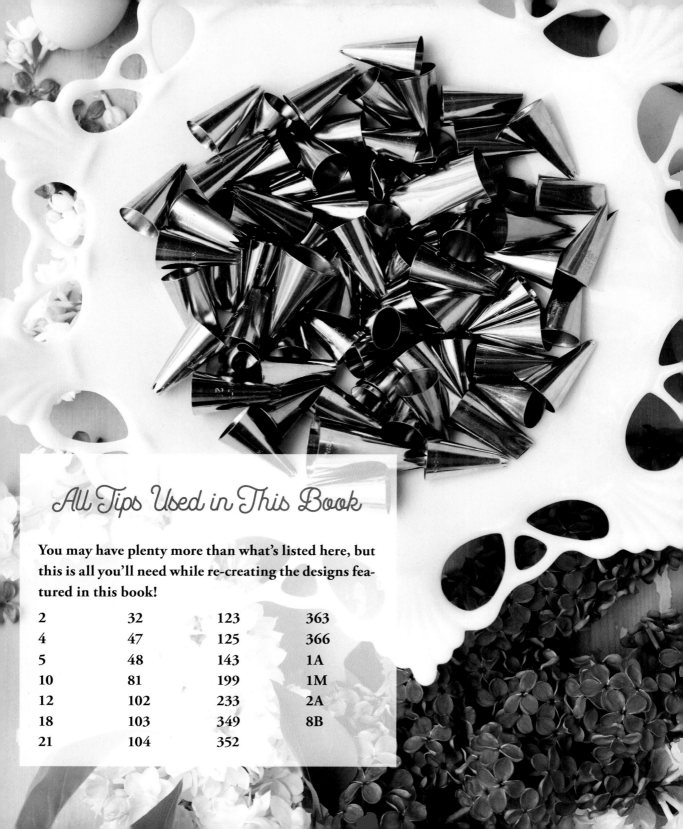

All Tips Used in This Book

You may have plenty more than what's listed here, but this is all you'll need while re-creating the designs featured in this book!

2	32	123	363
4	47	125	366
5	48	143	1A
10	81	199	1M
12	102	233	2A
18	103	349	8B
21	104	352	

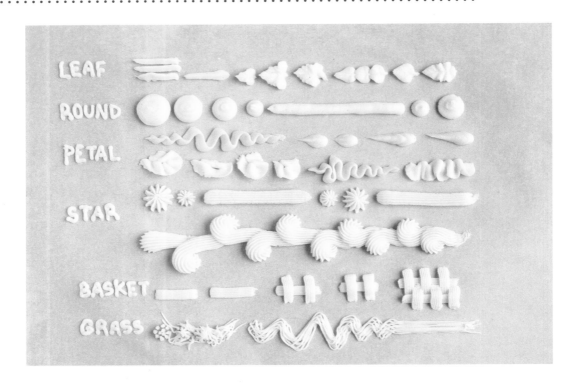

Piping 101

I use different sizes of each tip. The basics and most used are listed. I include instructions for piping each of these designs when used on each cookie throughout the book, but please use this page as a reference if you need more details on a certain style.

Rosette

To pipe a rosette, use a star tip and hold your bag straight up and down a little off the base of the cookie. Apply pressure and pipe down and then around in a circle and back down to connect. Decrease pressure as you connect. Stop pressure and pull away.

Leaf

Use a leaf tip at a slight 45-degree angle and the two points of the tip will be vertical; I call it the beak because that's what you want it to look like. Squeeze to make a base of the leaf. You will see the

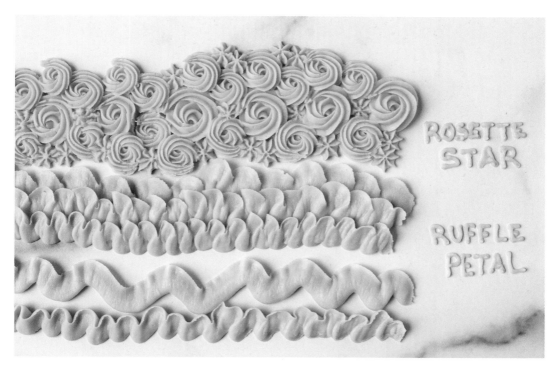

buttercream billow out the sides. Slowly pull upward to form the leaf and stop squeezing where you want the leaf to stop. Pull away.

Petal

Hold the bag so your wide end of the tip is at the base of your cookie. The skinny side will be at a 45-degree angle. You will apply pressure and squeeze while rounding your wrist in a half circle to make the petal.

Ruffle

The wide end of the tip will be touching your cookie base and the skinny end will be facing away from the cookie. Move your wrist up and down slightly to create the first ruffle. Repeat this motion until your ruffle is complete.

Star

Hold the piping bag straight up and the tip just above the surface of the cookie. Squeeze bag to form a star. Use light pressure for a small star and use a lot of pressure to make a larger star. Stop squeezing and then pull up to break the buttercream.

Coloring Buttercream—Master Tips

I find it helpful to mix in small batches. Mix 1 cup to desired shade.

- Use gel food coloring because it's more vibrant. Use liquid food coloring where noted.
- For red, use Wilton's no-taste red gel with crimson/color C in the Color Right system.
- For white, use Wilton's White-White icing color. Use a toothpick to get a little purple gel and add it into the buttercream; it sounds strange, but it will whiten the buttercream and counteracts with the yellow tint of the butter.
- For black buttercream, use Super Black by Americolor.
- The rest of the colors listed in my instructions can be any brand. I like Wilton and Americolor best.

To get deep and vibrant colors, mix to shade, cover with plastic wrap, and let it sit on the counter. The red, for example, will turn to a deep red. I do this with blues, reds, blacks, browns, and greens. Any color will deepen.

With flooding buttercream, you can color before or after. The heating process will make the shade a tad darker. If you want to make a dam and then flood, I suggest heating the buttercream halfway, pouring some in a tipless bag, and that will be your dam consistency. Heat the buttercream a little more and that will be your flood.

Coloring buttercream can be difficult, so start with a drop and add more. The more you experiment, the more color variations you will come up with. I use so many different brands and shades, a color chart was impossible to put together for you (though I tried!).

Recipes

These recipes have been tested and retested in my kitchen. I have tried to roll out any bumps in the dough for you. It's very important to read through the full ingredient list, instructions, and Master Tips before you start, as they all contain important information that will help make things flow easier for you.

Temperature and humidity can factor into your recipe. You may need to subtract or add a little flour depending on where you're located. I included a helpful chart in the back of the book because I'm sweet like that. (I'm just being silly, of course, but I really am invested in people who support me and love my recipes, so helping you be successful brings me joy.)

I know that Google will tell you different gram measurements if you try to convert cups to grams on your own; the numbers I've provided are what I've used and found success with. When measuring by weight, the grams can vary; I specifically measured per recipe numerous times and some have just a tad more or less flour. (I am measuring in high humidity, by the way.)

Remember to use the scoop-and-level method (page 11) when measuring flour. You don't want a dry cookie or a cookie that won't hold its shape. The dough will crumble if you've added too much.

Note: These sugar cookies are developed with the intent that they will be frosted with sweet buttercream. If they seem a little less sweet than you're used to, that's why. A few recipes I've included are great on their own because they are a little sweeter, like the Brown Butter (page 55), Raspberry (page 91), and Cookies & Cream (page 67). Keep that in mind. You can always add or subtract ¼ cup of sugar depending on the recipe and your preference. Everyone has a different palate for how sweet they like their cookies.

Don't knead the dough or overmix—that can lead to a hard cookie.

Another note: If you notice your oven is overbaking your cookies and they are browning too quickly on the bottom, reduce temperature from 375°F to 350°F and bake for 9 to 11 minutes instead.

I don't want you to give up on the first try, or even the second! I want you to try three, maybe even four times before you throw in your piping bag. If you've never baked cookies before, please remember that everyone has to start somewhere. Take a deep breath, reread How to Use This Book (page 9), the Master Tips, and all instructions before beginning!

Vanilla Almond Sugar Cookie

Makes 24 cookies

We can't have a new cookie book without a sugar cookie. Although this isn't my classic sugar cookie recipe, I think you will enjoy the hint of almond in this one and it's a tiny bit sweeter than my classic. You can absolutely leave out the almond. You'll find my classic sugar cookie recipe in my first book, Creative Cookie Decorating. I love the texture of a granulated sugar cookie, but I love the taste of an all-powdered-sugar sugar cookie, so I married them. This way your cookies stay nice and soft, and you get that classic sugar cookie taste, too. Remember to read the recipe, directions, and the Master Tips in their entirety before starting.

Ingredients

1 cup (227 grams) unsalted butter, softened
$^1/_2$ teaspoon (3 grams) salt
1 cup (200 grams) white granulated sugar
$^1/_2$ cup (60 grams) white confectioners' sugar, or powdered sugar
1 large egg (50 grams)
1 teaspoon (4 grams) pure vanilla extract
$^1/_4$–$^1/_2$ teaspoon (1–2 grams) almond extract
3 cups (375–390 grams) all-purpose flour, plus extra for rolling
$^1/_2$ teaspoon (2.5 grams) aluminum-free baking powder

Instructions

1. Cream butter and salt in a stand mixer with paddle attachment for 30 seconds on medium speed.

2. Mix in both sugars, and cream for 1 minute on medium speed.

3. Crack your egg in a small bowl to prevent shells in your dough and add into mix along with the vanilla and almond extracts. Cream together about 30 seconds on medium speed to fluff the butter and sugars together just until combined.

Continued on next page

4. Mix dry ingredients (flour and baking powder) in a separate bowl with a whisk. You can also sift dry ingredients. Then, add dry ingredients to wet ingredients.

5. Cover mixer with a towel to keep the flour mess in the mixing bowl. Mix on low speed; your dough will seem dry but it will all come together. It may take 2 minutes for the dough to form, so just keep mixing. The dough will start pulling off the sides once it's combined. Remember, this will take a minute. If you're using a hand mixer, you will have to press dough together once flour is all mixed in.

6. Preheat oven to 375°F. Lay out a sheet of plastic wrap, place dough on top, and form it into a disc shape to allow dough to chill quicker. Wrap up and place in refrigerator for at least 15 minutes to allow dough to firm up a little to prevent spreading. Line a cookie sheet with parchment paper or use a restaurant-grade aluminum baking sheet.

7. Flour your surface. I gently press my dough on the clean surface to make the flour stick before I add my flour. If you run your hand across the top of your rolled dough, you can feel any bumps or slightly raised areas. To get even dough, roll slowly up, down, and then to the sides. Roll dough out to a ¼-inch thick minimum and cut your cookies into desired shapes.

8. Place on a baking sheet about 2 inches apart and bake for 6 to 8 minutes, or until the cookie puffs up and the center looks matte.

9. Once baked, if there is any part of the cookie that needs a quick reshape, tighten up the cookies by gently pressing the sides of the cookie back into shape using an offset spatula. They will grow a little but shouldn't spread. Let sit for 1 minute on the cookie sheet to firm up. Then transfer to a cooling rack.

MASTER TIPS

Freeze bare cookies for a couple hours/overnight. I prefer to freeze the cookies overnight because it gives them added moisture to keep them soft. Pull cookies out of freezer 1 hour before frosting them.

Mix the salt with your wet ingredients so the salt dissolves through the dough better; we don't want crunchy salt granules in this cookie. If you can find Salted Sweet Cream Butter, I suggest using that and omitting salt altogether because it has the perfect amount of salt for these cookies. The cornstarch will help keep nice, crisp edges; I recommend using it.

Thick cookies balance out the sweetness of the buttercream, so don't make them thinner than ¼ inch. Frosted cookies can also be frozen for a week or two before your event.

If you want to freeze them, be gentle and treat them like frosted cupcakes until they crust over. When you pull them out of the freezer, be sure to allow the buttercream to crust back over.

If you cream your butter and sugars too much, it can lead to slight cracks in the baked cookie, so cream as instructed.

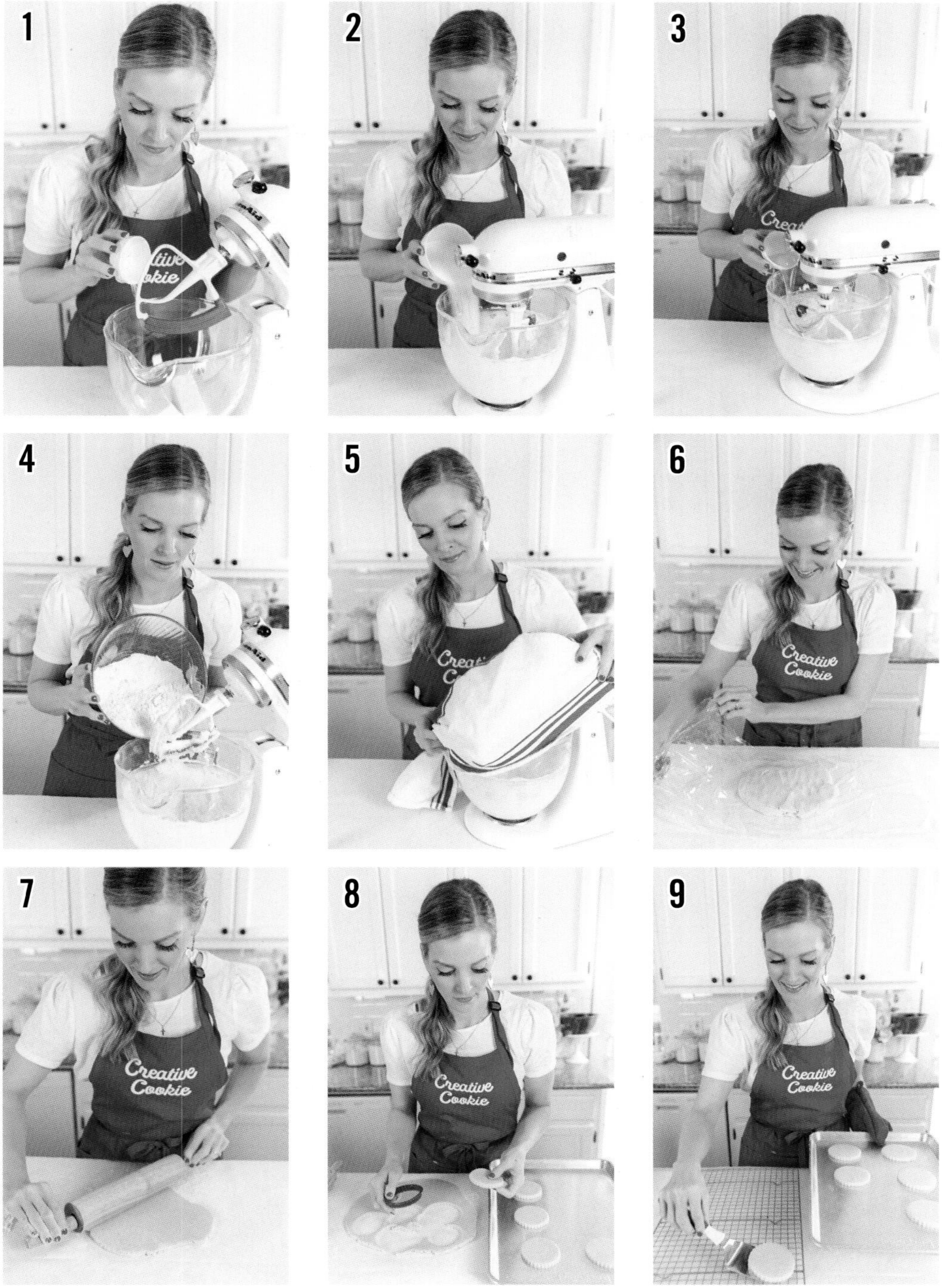
1
2
3
4
5
6
7
8
9
Creative Cookie

Thick Sugar Cookies

Makes 18–24 cookies

These soft, thick cookies pair beautifully with my flower cookies because they balance out the sweetness of the buttercream. These are thick cookies with sharp edges. The cream cheese smooths out the flavor and helps bind the dough to make it sturdy. You get a sugar cookie bite with the creaminess of the cream cheese that makes this one of my favorite new cookies to bake. They are so soft and delicious.

Ingredients

1 cup (227 grams) unsalted butter, softened
1/2 teaspoon (3 grams) salt
1 cup (200 gram) white granulated sugar
1/2 cup (60 grams) white confectioners' sugar, or powdered sugar
1/4 cup (60 grams or 2 ounces) cream cheese, softened
1 large egg (50 grams)
2 teaspoons (8 grams) pure vanilla extract
3 cups (375–390 grams) all-purpose flour, plus extra for rolling
1/2 teaspoon (2.5 grams) aluminum-free baking powder
2 tablespoons (15 grams) cornstarch

Instructions

1. Cream butter and salt in a stand mixer with paddle attachment for 30 seconds on medium speed.

2. Mix in both sugars and cream cheese. Cream for 1 minute on medium speed.

3. Crack your egg in a small bowl to prevent shells in your dough and add into mix along with the vanilla. Cream together about 30 seconds on medium speed just until incorporated.

4. Mix dry ingredients (flour, baking powder, and cornstarch) in a separate bowl with a whisk. You can also sift dry ingredients. Then, add dry ingredients to wet ingredients.

5. Cover with a kitchen towel, mix on low speed; your dough will seem dry, but it will all come together. It may take 2 minutes for the dough to form, so just keep mixing. The dough will start pulling off the sides once it's combined.

Continued on next page

6. Preheat oven to 350°F. Lay out a sheet of plastic wrap, place dough on top, and form it into a disc shape to allow dough to chill quicker. Wrap up and place in refrigerator for at least 15 minutes for dough to firm up a little to prevent spreading. Line a cookie sheet with parchment paper or lay bare on a restaurant-grade aluminum baking sheet.

7. Flour your surface. To get even dough, roll slowly up, down, and then to the sides. Roll dough out to a ⅜-inch thick minimum, and cut your cookies into desired shapes.

8. Place baking sheet about 2 inches apart and bake for 10 to 11 minutes, or until the cookie puffs up and the center looks matte.

9. Once baked, let sit for 1 minute on the cookie sheet to firm up. Then transfer to a cooling rack.

MASTER TIPS

These cookies are thick and meant for a buttercream design with more frosting, such as a flower cookie.

For help with rolling, I gently press my dough on the clean surface to make the flour stick before I add my flour. If you run your hand across the top of your rolled dough, you can feel any bumps or slightly raised areas.

Frost cookies once completely cooled or freeze bare cookies for a couple hours/overnight. I prefer to freeze the cookies overnight because it gives them added moisture to keep them soft. Pull cookies out of freezer 1 hour before frosting them.

Vanilla Bean Sugar Cookies

Makes 24 cookies

The tiny flecks in the vanilla bean cookie make a bare cookie so beautiful to look at. This recipe has both bean and extract for a wonderfully delicious vanilla flavor.

I have been using vanilla beans from a company that farms premium Guatemalan vanilla beans. It's good fun because I went to high school with the owner. I love when life comes full circle. Use premium vanilla beans and a very sharp knife to open the pod and scrape out all of those lovely beans

Ingredients

1 cup (227 grams) unsalted butter, softened
1/4 teaspoon (1.5 grams) salt
3/4 cup (150 grams) white granulated sugar
1/2 cup (60 grams) white confectioners' sugar, or powdered sugar
1 whole vanilla bean
1 teaspoon (4 grams) pure vanilla extract
1 large egg (50 grams)
3 cups (375–390 grams) all-purpose flour, plus extra for rolling
1/2 teaspoon (2.25 grams) aluminum-free baking powder

Instructions

1. Cream butter and salt in a stand mixer with paddle attachment for 30 seconds on medium speed.

2. Mix in both sugars and cream for 1 minute on medium speed. We don't want to add too much air to the dough or the tops of the cookie will crack in the baking process as the air escapes.

3. On a cutting board or parchment paper, take vanilla bean and a sharp knife and cut down the pod longways. Open the pod and expose the tiny black vanilla beans inside. Gently scrape the beans out and add them to the dough. Scrape the entire pod, being careful not to scrape down too far into the pod itself.

4. Next add in vanilla extract and egg. Cream together for about 30 seconds on medium, just until combined.

5. Mix dry ingredients (flour and baking powder) in a separate bowl with a whisk. You can also sift the dry ingredients. Then, add dry ingredients to wet ingredients.

Continued on next page

6. Mix on low speed; your dough will seem dry, but it will all come together. It may take 2 minutes for the dough to form, so just keep mixing. The dough will start pulling off the sides once it's combined.

7. Preheat oven to 375°F. Lay out a sheet of plastic wrap, place dough on top, and form it into a disc shape to allow dough to chill quicker. Wrap and place in refrigerator for at least 15 minutes to allow dough to firm up a little to prevent spreading. Line a cookie sheet with parchment paper or prepare to lay bare on a restaurant-grade aluminum baking sheet.

8. Flour your surface. To get even dough, roll slowly up, down, and then to the sides. Roll dough out to a ¼-inch thick minimum and cut your cookies into desired shapes.

9. Place on a baking sheet about 2 inches apart, and bake for 6 to 8 minutes, or until the cookie puffs up and the center looks matte.

10. Once baked, let sit for 1 minute on the cookie sheet to firm up. Then transfer to a cooling rack.

MASTER TIPS

Freeze bare cookies for a couple hours/overnight. I prefer to freeze the cookies overnight because it gives them added moisture to keep them soft. Pull cookies out of freezer 1 hour before frosting them.

Add 1 teaspoon of vanilla bean paste in place of the vanilla bean.

Adding 1 tablespoon of cornstarch can help cookies keep a straighter edge.

Brown Butter Cookies

Makes 24 cookies

Brown butter tastes like toffee, a little sweet and savory with a nutty flavor that comes through when the butter is nicely browned. The butter will lose a little of its volume because some of the moisture will evaporate. The marvelous taste and the toasted aroma of brown butter will fill your senses and deepen the flavor of your cookies, which will easily please any cookie lover. It's a distinct flavor unlike any other that will make you salivate even before the cookies are baked.

Browning butter is simple, but you must keep an eye on the butter, or it will burn. It's more of a gentle cooking process that will take about 5 minutes on medium heat. Instructions are included in this recipe. See photo to understand what you're looking for with the browned butter. (If the pan were lighter, you could see more of the brown bits.)

Ingredients

1 cup (227 grams) unsalted butter, softened and browned
1/4 teaspoon plus a big pinch (2.25 grams) salt
3/4 cup (90 grams) powdered confectioners› sugar
1/2 cup (100 grams) white granulated sugar
1/4 cup (60 grams or 2 ounces) cream cheese
1 large egg (50 grams)
1 1/2 teaspoons (6 grams) pure vanilla extract
2 1/2 cups (320–330 grams) all-purpose flour, plus extra for rolling
1 teaspoon (5 grams) aluminum-free baking powder
2 tablespoons (15 grams) cornstarch

Instructions

1. In a large pan over medium heat, add butter and use a wooden spoon or rubber spatula to stir. The butter will begin to foam and may sizzle a bit around the edges. Keep stirring; the process will take 5 to 6 minutes, longer if you don't see the milk fats at the bottom of the pan start to turn golden brown. Pour into a heat-safe bowl and chill in the refrigerator or freezer until cold and solid—make sure to stir the liquid frequently to ensure the brown bits don't clump together on the bottom.

2. After it's chilled, use a rubber spatula to remove the butter and put it into a stand mixer. Beat on medium speed for 1 minute so the brown bits will be evenly distributed.

Continued on next page

3. Mix in both sugars and cream cheese, and mix for about 30 seconds on medium speed.

4. Crack your egg in a small bowl to prevent shells in your dough and add into mix along with the vanilla. Cream together about 30 seconds on medium speed just to incorporate everything.

5. Mix or sift dry ingredients (flour, baking powder, and cornstarch) with a whisk in a separate bowl. Then, add dry ingredients to wet ingredients.

6. Mix on low speed. The dough will start pulling off the sides once it's combined. It may seem dry, but keep mixing for a minute and it will come together.

7. Preheat oven to 375°F. Lay out a sheet of plastic wrap, turn dough out on plastic, and form it into a disc shape to allow dough to chill quicker. Wrap and place in refrigerator for at least 15 minutes to allow dough to firm up a little to prevent spreading. Line a cookie sheet with parchment paper or prepare to lay bare on a restaurant-grade aluminum baking sheet.

8. Flour your surface. If you run your hand across the top of your rolled dough, you can feel any bumps or slightly raised areas. To get even dough, roll slowly up, down, and then to the sides evenly. Roll dough out to a ¼-inch thick minimum and cut your cookies into desired shapes.

9. Place on a baking sheet 2 inches or more apart, and bake for 6 to 8 minutes, or until the cookie puffs up and the center doesn't look really shiny (also called matte). Add an extra minute if cookies are overly shiny and wet-looking after they puff up.

10. Once baked, let sit for 1 minute on the cookie sheet to firm up. Then transfer to a cooling rack.

MASTER TIP

Keep an eye on the browned butter. It will burn fast if it's not removed from heat just after the fats brown at the bottom. Keep stirring. Don't be intimidated. It's a very easy process; you just have to keep stirring.

Black Velvet Cookies

Makes 24 cookies

Doesn't the title intrigue you?! Black velvet cacao or cocoa are the same thing; it's a silky black, smooth, Dutch-processed powder that is dutched further so the color and flavor are deeper with no acidity in the chocolate. An Oreo cookie is made with black velvet cacao powder—just to give you an idea! I found my black cacao online, and you should be able to, too!

Ingredients

1 cup (227 grams) unsalted butter, softened
1/4 teaspoon plus a big pinch (2.25 grams) salt
3/4 cup (150 grams) white granulated sugar
1/2 cup (60 grams) white confectioners' sugar, or powdered sugar
1 large egg (50 grams)
1 teaspoon (4 grams) pure vanilla extract
2 2/3 cups (355 grams) all-purpose flour, plus extra for rolling
1 teaspoon (5 grams) aluminum free baking powder
1/2 cup (45 grams) black velvet premium processed cacao powder

Instructions

1. Cream butter, salt, and sugars together in a stand mixer on medium speed for 1 minute.

2. Add in egg and vanilla, and mix together for 30 more seconds.

3. Mix dry ingredients (flour, baking powder, and cacao powder) in separate bowl. I use a whisk to blend the dry ingredients together. You could also sift them.

4. Add dry ingredients to your wet ingredients. Mix until a dough forms and pulls away from the sides of the bowl.

5. Remove dough from bowl and turn it out on a piece of plastic wrap. Flatten like a disc, wrap, and place in fridge for at least 30 minutes. If you flatten the dough, it gets colder quickly.

6. Preheat oven to 375°F.

7. Flour your surface and roll dough out to 1/4-inch thick. Cut your cookies out into desired shapes. The flour will bake off of the chocolate cookies.

Continued on next page

8. Place cookies straight onto an aluminum, restaurant-grade baking sheet or nonstick baking sheet lined with parchment paper, and bake for 6 to 7 minutes, or until the cookie puffs up and the top appears matte. These will bake quickly, so keep an eye out.

9. Once baked, let sit for 1 minute on the cookie sheet to firm up. Transfer to a cooling rack so they can cool completely.

MASTER TIP

Freeze baked cookies overnight to make them extra soft. Pull them out in the morning and frost. Add in mint extract for a minty chocolate cookie, perfect for St. Patrick's Day. I used WG Black Velvet Cocoa Powder Premium Dutched, which can easily be found online.

Gingerbread Cut-Out Cookies

Makes 24 cookies

Is there anything better than the smell of gingerbread baking in the oven? It brings me right back to my childhood, baking in the kitchen with my grandma. These cookies are nice and thick and keep their shape very well. They are perfectly chewy, spiced, and brown-sugared to holiday deliciousness. The buttercream frosting adds a creamy sweetness you won't want to leave off, but if you're in a pinch, simply add cinnamon imperials or sprinkles before baking.

Ingredients

1 cup (227 grams) unsalted butter, softened
1/4 teaspoon plus a big pinch (2.25 grams) salt
3/4 cup (165 grams) firmly packed dark brown sugar
1/4 cup (50 grams) white granulated sugar
1 large egg (50 grams)
1 1/2 teaspoons (6 grams) pure vanilla extract
1/4 cup (85 grams) unsulphured molasses
2 teaspoons (4 grams) ground cinnamon
1 teaspoon (2 grams) ground ginger
1/4 teaspoon ground nutmeg
1/8 teaspoon ground cloves
3 cups (375–390 grams) all-purpose flour, plus extra for rolling
1 teaspoon (5 grams) aluminum-free baking powder

Instructions

1. Cream butter and salt in a stand mixer with paddle attachment for 30 seconds.

2. Mix in both sugars. Cream for 1 minute on medium speed.

3. Crack your egg in a small bowl to prevent shells in your dough and add into mix along with the vanilla. Cream together about 30 seconds on medium speed to fluff the butter and sugars together. You don't need to aerate butter and sugars much.

4. Add molasses. Mix just until incorporated.

5. Mix or sift in dry ingredients (cinnamon, ginger, nutmeg, cloves, flour, and baking powder) in a separate bowl with a whisk. Then, add dry ingredients to wet ingredients.

Continued on next page

6. Mix on low speed. The dough will start pulling off the sides once it's combined. This dough will seem slightly stickier than the classic sugar cookie dough.

7. Preheat oven to 375°F. Lay out a sheet of plastic wrap, scoop dough on top, and form it into a disc shape to allow dough to chill quicker. Wrap and place in refrigerator for at least 15 minutes for dough to firm up a little to prevent spreading. Line a cookie sheet with parchment paper or prepare to lay bare on a restaurant-grade aluminum baking sheet.

8. Flour your surface. Roll dough out to ¼-inch thick minimum. Rolling between two sheets of parchment paper is effective, as well. If you run your hand across the top of your rolled dough, you can feel any bumps or slightly raised areas. To get even dough, roll slowly up, down, and then to the sides evenly. Cut your cookies into desired shapes.

9. Place on a baking sheet 2 inches or more apart, and bake for 6 to 8 minutes, or until the cookie puffs up and the center doesn't look really shiny. Add an extra minute if cookies are overly shiny and wet-looking after they puff up.

10. Once baked, let sit for 1 minute on the cookie sheet to firm up. Then transfer to a cooling rack.

MASTER TIPS

Don't skimp on the refrigeration. I take half of the dough and put the rest in the fridge while I'm rolling, so the half I'm not working with isn't sitting there, getting to room temperature.

For extra spice, add more cloves and nutmeg to the recipe.

White Chocolate Cinnamon Cut-Outs

Makes 24 large cookies

My daughter Reese inspired this recipe. She was telling me about a drink her coffee stand makes—a cinnamon-honey white chocolate mocha. This brown-sugary, soft, buttery cookie is enveloped in an aromatic cinnamon hug. It holds its shape and can be eaten with or without buttercream. Can you smell the sugar and cinnamon baking yet??? I can!

Ingredients

2 ounces (56 grams) of a quality white chocolate bar
1 cup (227 grams) unsalted butter, softened
$^1/_2$ teaspoon (3 grams) salt
$^3/_4$ cup (165 grams) firmly packed light brown sugar
$^1/_2$ cup (60 grams) powdered confectioners' sugar, or powdered sugar
1 large egg (50 grams)
1 teaspoon (4 grams) vanilla extract
3 cups (375–390 grams) all-purpose flour
1 teaspoon (5 grams) aluminum-free baking powder
1 teaspoon (2 grams) ground cinnamon

Instructions

1. Cut the bar into two, 2-ounce pieces. Reserve one for another batch of cookies later. Use a sharp knife and cut the white chocolate into small shards and pieces; this will help distribute the white chocolate through the dough. Set aside.

2. Cream butter and salt together for 1 minute in a stand mixer on medium speed to blend butter and salt together.

3. Add in sugars and mix on medium speed for about 30 seconds.

4. Add in egg and vanilla and mix just until combined.

5. Mix or sift dry ingredients (flour, baking powder, and cinnamon) in separate bowl. I use a whisk to blend the dry ingredients together.

6. Add dry ingredients to your wet ingredients. Mix until a dough forms and pulls away from the sides of the bowl and then add in white chocolate.

Continued on next page

7. Remove dough from bowl with a rubber spatula and wrap in plastic, place in fridge for at least 15 minutes. If you flatten the dough, it gets colder quickly. This will allow your dough to firm up a bit for rolling and getting sharp edges.

8. Preheat oven to 375°F.

9. Flour your surface and roll dough out to ¼ inch thick minimum. Cut your cookies into desired shapes.

10. Place on a baking sheet lined with parchment paper or straight onto a restaurant-grade aluminum baking sheet about 2 inches apart, and bake for 6 to 8 minutes, or just until the cookie puffs up and center is matte. Once baked, let sit for 1 minute on the cookie sheet to firm up.

11. Transfer to a cooling rack so they can cool completely.

MASTER TIP

I used a Lindt white chocolate bar, but you can use quality bakers' white chocolate. Always use high-quality chocolate when baking. If the dough is too sweet for you, reduce the amount of powdered sugar by ¼ cup. The white chocolate adds extra sweetness.

Cookies & Cream

Makes 24 large cookies

Just the title itself makes me drool. I love Oreos, so why not make them into a cookie that tastes like cookies n' cream ice cream? I use a little cream cheese in this recipe to give it an extra-creamy flavor. You will also notice that I'm using cornstarch. Cornstarch is a great thickener to help prevent spreading; it also keeps the cookies extra soft. My husband will tell you this is his new favorite cookie. Make sure to read the Master Tips before starting the recipe.

Ingredients

1 cup (227 grams) unsalted butter, softened
1/2 teaspoon (3 grams) salt
1 cup (200 grams) granulated sugar
1/4 cup (60 grams) or 2 ounces cream cheese, cold
1 large egg (50 grams)
1 1/2 teaspoons (6 grams) vanilla extract
3 cups (375–390 grams) all-purpose flour
1 tablespoon (7.5 grams) cornstarch
1 teaspoon (5 grams) aluminum-free baking powder
1 cup (150 grams) crushed Oreo cookies, about 10 cookies

Instructions

1. Cream butter and salt together in a stand mixer on medium speed for about 30 minutes.

2. Add in sugar and cream cheese and mix for 1 minute on medium speed. Scrape down sides halfway through if you have to.

3. Add in egg and vanilla, and mix until creamy. About 30 more seconds.

4. Mix or sift dry ingredients (flour, cornstarch, and baking powder) in separate bowl. I use a whisk to blend the dry ingredients together.

5. Add dry ingredients to your wet ingredients. Mix until a dough forms and it pulls away from the sides of the bowl. It will be sticky.

6. In a food processor, crumble Oreo cookies. You can also use a thick plastic bag and rolling pin to crush the Oreos. Add them into dough.

Continued on page 69

7. Remove dough from bowl with a rubber spatula, wrap in plastic, and place in fridge for at least 15 minutes, or more. If you flatten the dough into a disc shape, it gets colder quickly. This will allow your dough to firm up a bit for rolling and getting sharp edges.

8. Preheat oven to 375°F. Flour your surface and roll dough out to ¼-inch thick minimum. Cut your cookies into desired shapes.

9. Place on an restaurant-grade aluminum baking sheet or nonstick baking sheet lined with parchment paper about 2 inches apart and bake for 7 to 9 minutes, or just until the cookie puffs up and the center is matte.

10. Once baked, let sit for 1 minute on the cookie sheet to firm up. Then, transfer to a cooling rack so they can cool completely.

MASTER TIPS

Softened means out of the fridge for 30 minutes to an hour. Do not put butter in the microwave. You should be able to press a finger indent in the butter but not smoosh it.

It's very important to chill for the time listed so your cookies hold their shape. They will grow a tiny bit but should not spread.

Golden Cookies

Makes 24 large cookies

This recipe is like my Cookies & Cream but with Golden Oreos. These are delicious on their own, but I'm always up for adding frosting to baked goods. The golden cookies have a bright vanilla flavor that adds a sweet, creamy flavor to the cookies.

Ingredients

1 cup (227 grams) unsalted butter, softened
$1/2$ teaspoon (3 grams) salt
$3/4$ cup (150 grams) granulated sugar
$1/4$ cup (60 grams or 2 ounces) cream cheese, cold
1 large egg (50 grams)
$1/2$ teaspoon (2 grams) pure vanilla extract
3 cups (375–390 grams) all-purpose flour
1 tablespoon (7.5 grams) cornstarch
1 teaspoon (5 grams) aluminum-free baking powder
1 cup (150 grams) crushed Golden Oreo cookies, about 10 cookies

Instructions

1. Cream butter and salt together in a stand mixer with paddle attachment for 1 minute.

2. Add in sugar and cream cheese and mix on medium speed for about 30 seconds.

3. Add in egg and vanilla, and mix until creamy, about 30 more seconds.

4. Mix or sift dry ingredients (flour, cornstarch, and baking powder) in a separate bowl. I use a whisk to blend the dry ingredients together.

5. Add dry ingredients to your wet ingredients. Mix until a dough forms. It will be sticky.

6. In a food processor, pulse Oreo cookies. You can also use a thick plastic bag and rolling pin to crush the Oreos. Add them into dough and mix just until combined.

7. Remove dough from bowl with a rubber spatula and wrap in plastic, then place in fridge for at least 30 minutes. If you flatten the dough into a disc shape, it will cool faster. This will allow your dough to firm up a bit for rolling and getting sharp edges.

8. Preheat oven to 375°F.

Continued on next page

9. Flour your surface and roll dough out to ¼-inch thick minimum. Cut your cookies into desired shapes.

10. Place about 2 inches apart on an aluminum restaurant-grade baking sheet or nonstick baking sheet lined with parchment paper, and bake for 7 to 9 minutes, or just until the cookie puffs up and the center is matte. Keep an eye on them.

11. Once baked, let sit for 1 minute on the cookie sheet to firm up. Transfer to a cooling rack so they can cool completely.

MASTER TIPS

Use any flavor of Oreo cookie for a delicious treat. Chill longer if you live in a very warm climate.

Latte Sugar Cookies

Makes 18–24 cookies

Here, we have a delicious marriage of two sugars and espresso powder that gives the cookie an extra special taste. I love when desserts have a hint of coffee flavoring, but my husband would not agree with me. If you don't like coffee in desserts, this cookie isn't for you. Just the smell of these baking makes me happy.

Ingredients

1 cup (227 grams) unsalted butter, softened
1/2 teaspoon salt (3 grams)
1/2 cup (100 grams) white granulated sugar
1/2 cup (165 grams) firmly packed light brown sugar
1 large egg (50 grams)
2 teaspoons (8 grams) pure vanilla extract
1 teaspoon (3 grams) teaspoon espresso powder for baking
3 cups (375–390 grams) all-purpose flour, plus extra for rolling
1 teaspoon (5 grams) aluminum-free baking powder

Instructions

1. Cream butter and salt in a stand mixer with paddle attachment for 30 seconds on medium speed.

2. Mix in both sugars and cream for 1 minute on medium speed.

3. Crack your egg in a small bowl to prevent shells in your dough and add into mix along with the vanilla. Cream together about 30 seconds on medium speed or just until incorporated.

4. Then mix dry ingredients (espresso powder, flour, and baking powder) in a separate bowl with a whisk. You can also sift them if you'd like. Then, add dry ingredients to wet ingredients.

5. Mix on low speed; your dough will seem dry, but it will all come together. The dough will start pulling off the sides once it's combined—this is when you stop mixing. Overmixing will cause a hard cookie.

6. Preheat oven to 375°F.

Continued on next page

7. Lay out a sheet of plastic wrap, place dough on top, and form it into a disc shape to allow dough to chill quicker. Wrap and place in refrigerator for at least 15 minutes for dough to firm up a little to prevent spreading. Line a cookie sheet with parchment paper or prepare to lay bare on a restaurant-grade aluminum baking sheet.

8. Flour your surface. To get even dough, roll slowly up, down, and then to the sides. Roll dough to ¼ inch-thick minimum and cut your cookies into desired shapes.

9. Place on sheet 2 inches apart, and bake for 6 to 8 minutes, or until the cookie puffs up and the center looks matte.

10. Once baked, let sit for 1 minute on the cookie sheet to firm up. Then transfer to a cooling rack.

MASTER TIP

Add an extra ½ teaspoon espresso powder for a rich flavor of espresso. I bought King Arthur Flour espresso powder online, and I love how it bakes.

Apple Cider Cookies
Makes 24 cookies

My son Nick has had a love for apple cider since I can remember (the packets mixed with hot water, specifically). So I thought, what would it taste like to add a packet of apple cider to cookie dough? I started mixing, and the sweet aroma of the apple cider and the rich brown sugar flavor brought me right to autumn. These baked up like a dream. They have a subtle tartness from the cider packet and a hint of caramel with the sugar—something we all need in our lives.

Ingredients

1 cup (227 grams) unsalted butter, softened
¼ teaspoon (1.5 grams) salt
1 cup (220 grams) firmly packed light brown sugar
1 packet apple cider mix (I use Alpine spiced apple cider)
1 large egg (50 grams)
1½ teaspoons (6 grams) pure vanilla extract
3 cups (375–390 grams) all-purpose flour, plus extra for rolling
1 teaspoon (5 grams) aluminum-free baking powder

Instructions

1. Cream butter and salt in a stand mixer with paddle attachment for 30 seconds on medium speed.

2. Mix in brown sugar and apple cider mix, and cream for 1 minute on medium speed.

3. Next add in egg and vanilla extract. Cream together about 30 seconds on medium until combined.

4. Mix dry ingredients (flour and baking powder) in a separate bowl with a whisk. You may also choose to sift them. Then, add dry ingredients to wet ingredients.

5. Mix on low speed; your dough will seem dry, but it will all come together. It may take 2 minutes for the dough to form, so just keep mixing. The dough will start pulling off the sides once it's combined, which is your signal to stop mixing.

6. Preheat oven to 375°F. Lay out a sheet of plastic wrap, place dough on top, and form it into a disc shape to allow dough to chill quicker. Wrap and place in refrigerator for at least 15 minutes to allow dough to firm up a little to prevent spreading.

Continued on next page

7. Line a cookie sheet with parchment paper or prepare to lay dough bare on a restaurant-grade aluminum baking sheet.

8. Flour your surface. To get even dough, roll slowly up, down, and then to the sides. Roll dough out to ¼-inch thick minimum and cut your cookies. Place about 2 inches apart, and bake for 6 to 8 minutes or when the cookie puffs up and the center looks matte.

9. Once baked, let sit for 1 minute on the cookie sheet to firm up. Then transfer to a cooling rack.

MASTER TIP

Add in finely chopped dried apples to give this cookie a deeper apple flavor.

Lemon Sugar Cookies

Makes 18–24 cookies

This cookie tastes like a lemon bar, but it's not too sweet, so it has a balance when butter-cream is added. It has a zingy, sweet, creamy, tart flavor with each bite. I feel like the summer months are calling while I smell these cookies baking. I could eat lemon desserts every day, so when this recipe turned out delicious, I was overjoyed and excited to share with my fellow lemon lovers.

Ingredients

1 cup (227 grams) unsalted butter, softened
1/2 teaspoon (3 grams) salt
3/4 cup (150 grams) white granulated sugar
1/2 cup (60 grams) white confectioners' sugar, or powdered sugar
1 large egg (50 grams)
1 teaspoon (4 grams) pure vanilla extract
Zest from 1 medium lemon
1 tablespoon (15 grams) lemon juice
3 cups (375–390 grams) all-purpose flour, plus extra for rolling
1 teaspoon (5 grams) aluminum-free baking powder

Instructions

1. Cream butter and salt in a stand mixer with paddle attachment for 30 seconds on medium speed.

2. Mix in both sugars and cream for 1 minute on medium speed.

3. Crack your egg in a small bowl to prevent shells in your dough and add into mix along with the vanilla. Add in lemon zest and juice, cream together about 30 seconds on medium speed just until incorporated.

4. Then mix dry ingredients (flour and baking powder) in a separate bowl with a whisk. You may also sift these. Then, add dry ingredients to wet ingredients.

5. Mix on low speed. The dough will start pulling off the sides once it's combined, which is your cue to stop mixing. Overmixing will cause a hard cookie.

Continued on next page

6. Preheat oven to 375°F. Lay out a sheet of plastic wrap, place dough on top, and form it into a disc shape to allow dough to chill quicker. Wrap and place in refrigerator for at least 15 minutes for dough to firm up a little to prevent spreading. Line a cookie sheet with parchment paper or prepare to lay bare on a restaurant-grade aluminum baking sheet.

7. Flour your surface. To get even dough, roll slowly up, down, and then to the sides. Roll dough out to ¼ inch thick minimum and cut your cookies into desired shapes.

8. Place on baking sheet about 2 inches apart, and bake for 6 to 8 minutes or until the cookie puffs up and the center looks matte.

9. Once baked, let sit for 1 minute on the cookie sheet to firm up. Then transfer to a cooling rack.

MASTER TIP

One medium lemon should give you 1 tablespoon of juice. Roll the lemon on the counter with the palm of your hand, firmly pressing, to loosen up the inside so the juice comes out easily. Zesting a lemon adds so much flavor because of the natural oils in the peel. Just remove the yellow color; don't zest into the pith or white part because that will be bitter. I use a microplane to zest. This makes a fine zest that incorporates into dough very well.

Toffee Brown Sugar Cookies

Makes 24 large cookies

This cookie is a stand-alone cookie and doesn't need frosting but isn't too sweet to add buttercream to. I prefer them with buttercream. The rich, brown sugar, caramel flavor complements the Heath bar and chocolate chips for a sweet treat. The butter really comes through in these cookies. They stay soft and delicate but don't fall apart when buttercream is added.

Ingredients

1 cup (225 grams) unsalted butter, softened
1/2 teaspoon (3 grams) salt
1 cup (220 grams) firmly packed light brown sugar
1 large egg (50 grams)
1 teaspoon (4 grams) pure vanilla extract
3 cups (375–390 grams) all-purpose flour
1 teaspoon (5 grams) baking powder
1/3 cup (54 grams) Heath bar bits
1/3 cup (56 grams) mini semisweet chocolate chips

Instructions

1. Cream butter and salt together in a stand mixer on medium speed for 1 minute to incorporate the butter and salt.

2. Add in sugar and mix again for 1 minute, medium speed.

3. Crack egg in a separate small bowl to prevent shells getting into dough, then add it in to mix, along with vanilla.

4. Mix dry ingredients (flour and baking powder) in a separate bowl. I use a whisk to blend the dry ingredients together, but you may also choose to sift them.

5. Add dry ingredients to your wet ingredients. Mix until the dough forms and it pulls away from the sides of the bowl. Add in Heath bar bits and chocolate chips, then mix again to incorporate.

6. Remove dough from bowl with a rubber spatula, wrap in plastic, and place in the fridge for at least 15 minutes. If you flatten the dough, it gets colder quickly. This will allow your dough to firm up a bit for rolling and getting sharp edges.

Continued on next page

7. Preheat oven to 375°F.

8. Flour your surface and roll dough out to ¼-inch thick minimum. Cut your cookies into desired shapes.

9. Place about 2 inches apart on a baking sheet lined with parchment paper or straight on a restaurant-grade aluminum baking sheet, and bake for 6 to 8 minutes, or until the cookie puffs up and center is matte. Once baked, let sit for 1 minute on the cookie sheet to firm up.

10. Transfer to a cooling rack so they can cool completely.

MASTER TIP

Roll cookies to ³/₈ inch for a thick, delicious cookie. Drizzle on Glaze (page 133) or dip halfway in chocolate.

Peanut Butter Cut-Outs

Makes 24 large cookies

I'm a huge fan of peanut butter, especially when it's married with buttercream frosting. This has the perfect amount of nuttiness with a little sweet; it's not too sugary, so when the cookie is coupled with buttercream, it tastes perfect. It's very important to know that the cookies can be crumbly if you overbake, so bake time and measurements are crucial to ensure they are soft and not dry. This recipe is a must-bake from this book!!

Ingredients

1 cup (227 grams) unsalted butter, softened
¼ teaspoon (1.5 grams) salt
½ cup (100 grams) granulated sugar
½ cup (110 grams) brown sugar
1 large egg (50 grams)
2 teaspoons (8 grams) pure vanilla extract
½ cup (128 grams) creamy peanut butter
2½ cups (325 grams) all-purpose flour
1 tablespoon (7.5 grams) cornstarch

Instructions

1. Cream butter and salt together in a stand mixer on medium speed 1 minute to incorporate the salt into the butter.
2. Add in both sugars and mix for 1 minute on medium speed.
3. Add in egg, vanilla, and peanut butter and cream together for 30 more seconds.
4. Mix dry ingredients (flour and cornstarch) in separate bowl. I use a whisk to blend the dry ingredients together, but you may also choose to sift them.
5. Add dry ingredients to your wet ingredients. Mix until a dough forms. It will seem a little dry, but it will all come together.
6. Remove dough from bowl, wrap in plastic, and place in fridge for at least 15 minutes. If you flatten the dough, it gets colder quickly.
7. Preheat oven to 375°F.

Continued on page 87

8. Lightly flour your surface and roll dough out to ¼-inch thick. Cut your cookies into desired shapes.

9. Use a restaurant-grade aluminum cookie sheet or line a nonstick cookie sheet with parchment paper to prepare for cookies. Place cookies about 2 inches apart on the baking sheet, and bake for 6 to 8 minutes, or until the cookie puffs up nicely in the center. Don't overbake.

10. Let sit for 1 minute on the cookie sheet to firm up. Transfer to a cooling rack so they can cool completely.

MASTER TIPS

Peanut butter can dry out the cookies so be very careful not to overbake—I know I've said it three times, but it's necessary.

Rolling the dough thinner than ¼-inch thick will result in a crispy cookie. I prefer thick and soft baked cookies, but maybe you like that crunch!

Peppermint Sugar Cookies

Makes 24 large cookies

These peppermint sugar cookies take my tastebuds right to winter. The crisp, distinct taste of peppermint reminds me of peppermint bark that I hurry straight to the store and buy each and every holiday season. I am adding the cornstarch because it helps keep the cookies stable and tender, which really creates a melt-in-your-mouth bite. Don't overbake these cookies; let's keep them soft.

Ingredients

1 cup (227 grams) unsalted butter, softened
1/2 teaspoon (3 grams) salt
1 cup (200 grams) granulated sugar
1/2 cup (60 grams) powdered sugar
1 large egg (50 grams)
1 teaspoon (4 grams) pure vanilla extract
1/2 teaspoon (2 grams) peppermint extract
2 3/4 cups (365 grams) all-purpose flour
1/2 teaspoon (2.5 grams) aluminum-free baking powder
3 tablespoons (22.5 grams) cornstarch

Instructions

1. Cream butter and salt together in a stand mixer on medium speed for 30 seconds to incorporate the salt into the butter.

2. Add in both sugars and mix for 1 minute.

3. Add in egg, vanilla, and peppermint extract, and mix together just until incorporated.

4. Ina separate bowl, mix dry ingredients (flour, baking powder, and cornstarch) in separate bowl. I use a whisk to blend the dry ingredients together, but you may also choose to sift them.

5. Add dry ingredients to your wet ingredients. Mix until a dough forms and it pulls away from the sides of the bowl. It will seem a little dry, but it will all come together.

6. Remove dough from bowl, wrap in plastic, and place in fridge for at least 15 minutes. If you flatten the dough, it gets colder quickly.

Continued on next page

7. Preheat oven to 375°F.

8. Flour your surface and roll dough out to ¼ inch thick. Cut your cookies into desired shapes.

9. Place about 2 inches apart on an aluminum restaurant-grade baking sheet or nonstick baking sheet lined with parchment paper, and bake for 6 to 8 minutes, or until the cookie puffs up and its matte on the top.

10. Once baked, let sit for 1 minute on the cookie sheet to firm up then transfer to a cooling rack so they can cool completely.

MASTER TIP

Peppermint extract and mint extract are not one and the same. They are not interchangeable. Mint extract pairs wonderfully with chocolate; try adding ½ teaspoon to my Black Velvet Cookie recipe (page 57). For this one, only peppermint extract will do. Peppermint extract is very potent—don't overpour the extract.

Raspberry Sugar Cookies

Makes 18–24 cookies

This cookie tastes like a raspberry milkshake, fresh and creamy. You don't even have to add a ton of frosting to these delicious beauties. Drizzle with a little glaze or some flood consistency buttercream for a simple cookie that likes to show off its look. These cookies are bright and beautiful with that raspberry color.

Ingredients

1 cup (227 grams) unsalted butter, softened
$^1/_2$ teaspoon (3 grams) salt
$^3/_4$ cup (150 grams) white granulated sugar
$^1/_2$ cup (60 grams) white confectioners' sugar, or powdered sugar
1 large egg (50 grams)
$1^1/_2$ teaspoons (6 grams) pure vanilla extract
1 (1.3-ounce) bag freeze-dried raspberries
$2^1/_2$ cups (335 grams) all-purpose flour, plus extra for rolling
$^1/_2$ teaspoon (2.25 grams) aluminum-free baking powder

Instructions

1. Cream butter and salt in a stand mixer with paddle attachment for 30 seconds on medium speed.

2. Mix in both sugars and cream for 1 minute on medium speed.

3. Crack your egg in a small bowl to prevent shells in your dough and add into mix along with the vanilla. Cream together about 30 seconds on medium speed just until incorporated.

4. With a food processer, pulse freeze-dried raspberries into powder. This should measure a little more than ½ cup (56 grams). If you don't want seeds, now is the time to sift the powder.

5. Then mix dry ingredients (flour, baking powder, and freeze-dried raspberry powder) in a separate bowl with a whisk. You can sift these if you'd like. Then, add dry ingredients to wet ingredients.

6. Mix on low speed. Your dough will seem dry, but it will all come together. It may take 2 minutes for the dough to form, so just keep mixing. The dough will start pulling off the sides once it's combined, which is when you should stop mixing. Overmixing will cause a hard cookie.

Continued on page 93

7. Preheat oven to 375°F. Lay out a sheet of plastic wrap, place dough on top, and form it into a disc shape to allow dough to chill quicker. Wrap and place in refrigerator for at least 15 minutes to allow dough to firm up a little to prevent spreading. Line a cookie sheet with parchment paper or prepare to lay dough bare on a restaurant-grade aluminum baking sheet.

8. Flour your surface. To get even dough, roll slowly up, down, and then to the sides. Roll dough out to ¼-inch thick minimum and cut your cookies into desired shapes.

9. Place about 2 inches apart on sheet, and bake for 6 to 8 minutes, or until the cookie puffs up and the center looks matte.

10. Once baked, let sit for 1 minute on the cookie sheet to firm up. Then transfer to a cooling rack.

MASTER TIPS

I like raspberry seeds, so I keep them in my cookies. If you don't want the seeds in, simply sift after you've put the freeze-dried raspberries in the food processer and turned it to powder.

These cookies can brown quickly on the bottom so be sure not to overbake.

Pumpkin Spice Sugar Cookies

Makes 18–24 cookies

These wonderfully soft cut-out cookies are perfectly pumpkin spiced and full of fall flavor. When cinnamon is baking in the oven, the scent makes me think of my childhood when my mom or grandma would bake for the holidays. These cookies hold their shape and can be drizzled with glaze, white chocolate, or decorated with buttercream.

Ingredients

1 cup (227 grams) unsalted butter, softened
$1/2$ teaspoon (3 grams) salt
$1/2$ cup (100 grams) white granulated sugar
$1/2$ cup (110 grams) firmly packed light brown sugar
1 large egg (50 grams)
2 teaspoons (8 grams) pure vanilla extract
1 teaspoon (2 grams) ground cinnamon
$1/4$ teaspoon ground ginger
$1/4$ teaspoon ground cloves
a dash of ground nutmeg (optional)
3 cups (375–390 grams) all-purpose flour, plus extra for rolling
1 teaspoon (2.25 grams) aluminum-free baking powder

Instructions

1. Cream butter and salt in a stand mixer with paddle attachment for 30 seconds on medium speed.

2. Mix in both sugars and cream for 1 minute on medium speed.

3. Crack your egg in a small bowl to prevent shells in your dough and add it into the mix along with the vanilla. Also add in cinnamon, ginger, cloves, and nutmeg (optional), and cream together about 30 seconds on medium speed just until incorporated.

4. Then mix dry ingredients (flour and baking powder) in a separate bowl with a whisk. You may sift these if you'd like. Then, add dry ingredients to wet ingredients.

5. Mix on low speed. Your dough will seem dry, but it will all come together. It may take 2 minutes for the dough to form, so just keep mixing. The dough will start pulling off the sides once it's combined, which is when you should stop mixing. Overmixing will cause a hard cookie.

Continued on next page

6. Preheat oven to 375°F. Lay out a sheet of plastic wrap, place dough on top, and form it into a disc shape to allow dough to chill quicker. Wrap and place in refrigerator for at least 15 minutes for dough to firm up a little to prevent spreading. Line a cookie sheet with parchment paper or prepare to lay bare on a restaurant-grade aluminum baking sheet.

7. Flour your surface. To get even dough, roll slowly up, down, and then to the sides. Roll dough out to ¼-inch thick minimum and cut your cookies into desired shapes.

8. Place about 2 inches apart on sheet, and bake for 6 to 8 minutes, or until the cookie puffs up and the center looks matte.

9. Once baked, let sit for 1 minute on the cookie sheet to firm up. Then transfer to a cooling rack.

MASTER TIP

Add in 1½ teaspoons of pumpkin spice and omit the spices altogether to make things easier if you don't already have these spices in your kitchen.

Mocha Cut-Out Cookies

Makes 18–24 cookies

A.k.a, You Mocha Me Happy Cookies! These are the perfect balance of chocolate and espresso flavoring. The espresso powder adds a deeper flavor to the chocolate. I love how well it pairs with buttercream for a new and exciting flavor of cookie.

Ingredients

1 cup (227 grams) unsalted butter, softened
1/2 teaspoon (3 grams) salt
1/2 cup (100 grams) white granulated sugar
1/2 cup (110 grams) firmly packed light brown sugar
1 large egg (50 grams)
2 teaspoons (8 grams) pure vanilla extract
1 teaspoon (3 grams) espresso powder for baking
2 2/3 cups (355 grams) all-purpose flour, plus extra for rolling
1 teaspoon (5 grams) aluminum-free baking powder
1/2 cup (43 grams) unsweetened cocoa powder

Instructions

1. Cream butter and salt in a stand mixer with paddle attachment for 30 seconds on medium speed.

2. Mix in both sugars and cream for 1 minute on medium speed.

3. Crack your egg in a small bowl to prevent shells in your dough and add into mix along with the vanilla. Cream together about 30 seconds on medium speed or just until incorporated.

4. Then mix dry ingredients (espresso powder, flour, baking powder, and unsweetened cocoa powder) in a separate bowl with a whisk. Sift if you'd like. Then, add dry ingredients to wet ingredients.

5. Mix on low speed. Your dough will seem dry, but it will all come together. The dough will start pulling off the sides once it's combined, which is your signal to stop mixing. Overmixing will cause a hard cookie.

6. Preheat oven to 375°F.

Continued on next page

7. Lay out a sheet of plastic wrap, place dough on top, and form it into a disc shape to allow dough to chill quicker. Wrap and place in refrigerator for at least 15 minutes to allow dough to firm up a little to prevent spreading. Line a cookie sheet with parchment paper or prepare to lay dough on a bare restaurant-grade aluminum baking sheet.

8. Flour your surface. To get even dough, roll slowly up, down, and then to the sides. Roll dough out to ¼ inch thick minimum and cut your cookies into desired shapes.

9. Place dough about 2 inches apart on a sheet, and bake for 6 to 8 minutes, or until the cookie puffs up and the center looks matte.

10. Once baked, let sit for 1 minute on the cookie sheet to firm up. Then transfer to a cooling rack.

MASTER TIPS

You can add black velvet cocoa powder in place of regular unsweetened cocoa powder if you'd like. That will give the cookies a deep Oreo-like taste. I use Hershey's unsweetened cocoa powder for this recipe.

The cookies will get brown quickly so keep an eye on them. Even a little under-baked is good for these.

Chocolate Chip Mint Cookies

Makes 24 cookies

These have a subtle minty flavor that isn't overpowering. The chocolate chips make it taste like mint chocolate chip ice cream. The green food coloring can be left out for a sugar cookie look with the same taste. These are perfect for St. Patrick's Day or a cute ice cream–themed cookie set. Chocolate chip mint is one of those classics that we enjoy.

Ingredients

1 cup (227 grams) unsalted butter, softened
1/2 teaspoon (3 grams) salt
3/4 cup (90 grams) powdered confectioners' sugar
1/2 cup (100 grams) granulated sugar
1 large egg (50 grams)
1 1/2 teaspoons (6 grams) pure vanilla extract
1/2 to 1 teaspoon (2 to 4 grams) mint extract
3 cups (375–390 grams) all-purpose flour, plus extra for rolling
1/2 teaspoon (2.5 grams) aluminum-free baking powder
1/2 cup (86 grams) mini semisweet chocolate chips

Instructions

1. Cream butter and salt in a stand mixer with paddle attachment for 30 seconds on medium speed.

2. Mix in both sugars and cream for 1 minute on medium speed.

3. Add in egg, vanilla, and mint extract. Cream together for about 30 seconds on medium until combined.

4. Mix dry ingredients (flour and baking powder) in a separate bowl with a whisk. You can also sift dry ingredients. Then, add dry ingredients to wet ingredients.

5. Mix on low speed. Your dough will seem dry, but it will all come together. It may take 2 minutes for the dough to form, so just keep mixing. The dough will start pulling off the sides once it's combined, which means it's time to stop mixing.

6. Add in mini chocolate chips and mix just until incorporated.

Continued on next page

7. Preheat the oven to 375°F. Lay out a sheet of plastic wrap, place dough on top, and form it into a disc shape to allow dough to chill quicker. Wrap and place in the refrigerator for at least 15 minutes for dough to firm up a little to prevent spreading.

8. Line a cookie sheet with parchment paper or prepare to lay cookies on a bare restaurant-grade aluminum baking sheet.

9. Flour your surface. To get even dough, roll slowly up, down, and then to the sides. Roll dough out to ¼-inch thick minimum and cut your cookies into desired shapes.

10. Place cookies on a sheet about 2 inches apart, and bake for 6 to 8 minutes, or until the cookie puffs up and the center looks matte.

11. Once baked, let sit for 1 minute on the cookie sheet to firm up. Then transfer to a cooling rack.

MASTER TIP

Chop small pieces of dark chocolate to really make this cookie scream "mint chocolate chip"! The mini chocolate chips are essential because it will be easier for cutting out the cookies.

Chocolate Chip Cookie Cake

Serves 12–20, depending on the size of slice

Decadent, salty, and buttery with rich, brown-sugar sweetness—this is the perfect dessert to decorate. This isn't the cut-out cookie you're used to seeing, but it is a wonderful way to decorate on a large surface to celebrate someone special. Check out the Celebrations chapter (page 303) to see what I did with my cookie cake.

This Chocolate Chip Cookie Cake is a version of my chocolate chip cookies altered slightly to make a cake. The cake bakes longer and is a little chewier because the bake time is increased to account for the large cookie. This is made in a 10-inch springform pan. If you don't have one, you can use a large pie dish or cake pan. Add parchment for easy removal or serve right in the dish. Springform pans don't need parchment. Decorate with buttercream for a delicious party treat.

Ingredients

1 cup (227 grams) unsalted butter, cold
1 cup (220 grams) firmly packed light brown sugar
$1/4$ cup (50 grams) white granulated sugar
1 large egg (50 grams)
1 egg yolk (18 grams)
2 teaspoons (8 grams) pure vanilla extract
2 cups (265 grams) all-purpose flour
$3/4$ teaspoon (4.5 grams) salt
$1/2$ teaspoon (2.5 grams) baking soda
$1/4$ teaspoon (1.25 grams) aluminum-free baking powder
1 tablespoon (7.5 grams) cornstarch
$11/4$ cups (232 grams) semisweet chocolate chips

Instructions

1. Preheat oven to 350°F.
2. Use a cheese grater to grate the butter directly into your stand mixer bowl. Cream butter and both sugars for 2 minutes on medium high speed until fluffy and lighter in color.

Continued on next page

3. Crack eggs (1 whole and 1 yolk only) into a small bowl to prevent shells in your dough and add into mix along with the vanilla. Don't add 2 whole eggs or the cookie will have a cake-like texture.

4. Then mix dry ingredients (flour, salt, baking soda, baking powder, and cornstarch) in a separate bowl with a whisk. You may choose to sift these ingredients. Then, add dry ingredients to wet ingredients. Mix on low speed just until combined

5. Add in chocolate chips and gently mix—do not overmix cookie dough.

6. Press dough evenly into the springform pan. Smooth down top for an even surface before baking.

7. Bake on the middle oven rack for 25 to 30 minutes. The edges will be golden brown. Don't overbake. The cookie should be nice and soft but cooked.

8. Once baked, pull out the pan. Tap it by lifting it up and tapping it down on the counter a couple times so the air escapes, creating a dense and delicious cookie. Let cool in the pan for 10 minutes to firm up and then remove the springform from the edge and transfer it from the bottom of the pan to a cooling rack. Cool completely before frosting.

MASTER TIP

Add extra semisweet chocolate chips for a super chocolaty cookie. Decrease to $3/4$ cup for a not-so-chocolaty cookie cake. Swap out $1/2$ cup semisweet chocolate chips with butterscotch chips, peanut butter chips, or white chocolate chips. Add in nuts or toffee. I like to substitute white chocolate chips and dried cranberries for the chocolate for a holiday flavor. Chocolate chunks work great but make it harder to cut nice slices when you're serving this cookie cake. Dress it up with delicious buttercream.

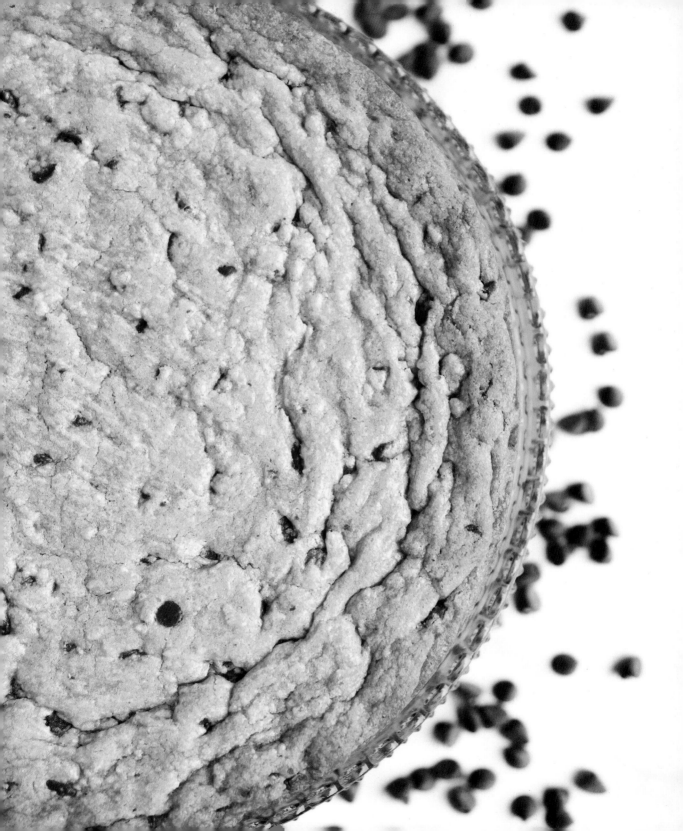

Sugar Cookie Cake

Serves 12–20, depending on the size of slice

A giant sugar cookie cake? Don't have to tell me twice. I'm in! This giant cookie cake will be a perfect addition to any party. Make this the center of attention on a table or a dessert spread. This cookie is buttery and soft with the right amount of sugar to keep the classic taste.

Ingredients

1 cup (227 grams) unsalted butter, cold
1/2 teaspoon (3 grams) salt
3/4 cup (150 grams) white granulated sugar
1/2 cup (60 grams) white confectioners' sugar, or powdered sugar
1 large egg (50 grams)
1 egg yolk (18 grams)
3 teaspoons (12 grams) pure vanilla extract
2 cups (265 grams) all-purpose flour
1/4 teaspoon (1.25 grams) baking soda
1/2 teaspoon (2.5 grams) aluminum-free baking powder
1 tablespoon cornstarch
1/4 cup multicolored nonpareils or 1/2 cup sprinkles

Instructions

1. Preheat oven to 350°F.
2. Use a cheese grater to grate the butter directly into the stand mixer bowl. Cream butter and salt in a stand mixer with paddle attachment for 30 seconds on medium speed.
3. Mix in both sugars and cream for 2 minutes on medium speed until fluffy and lighter in color.
4. Crack eggs (1 whole and 1 yolk only) into a small bowl to prevent shells in your dough and add into mix along with the vanilla. Don't add 2 whole eggs or the cookie will have a cake-like texture.
5. Then mix dry ingredients (flour, baking soda, baking powder, cornstarch) in a separate bowl with a whisk. You may sift these if you'd like. Then, add dry ingredients to wet ingredients.
6. Mix on low speed just until combined and add in sprinkles. Mix these in by hand.

Continued on next page

7. Press dough evenly into the springform pan. Smooth down top for an even surface before baking.

8. Bake on the middle oven rack for 25 to 30 minutes. The edges will be golden brown. Don't overbake. The cookie should be nice and soft but cooked.

9. Once baked, pull out the pan. Let cool in the pan for 10 minutes to firm up and then remove the springform from the edge and transfer it from the bottom of the pan to a cooling rack. Cool completely before frosting.

MASTER TIP

Stirring the sprinkles in by hand will prevent overmixing the dough and lessens the chances of the sprinkles bleeding.

Vegan Sugar Cookies

Makes 18–24 cookies

I'm not an expert in vegan baking, but I am a cookie expert, and I think these are absolutely delicious. So delicious, in fact, that your friends won't even know they're vegan. The soy buttery spread is the best I've found to bake with because it doesn't leave a strange aftertaste. Don't let allergy restrictions hold you back from living life to the fullest. You aren't really living unless you're enjoying delicious cookies! Let's get to it!

Ingredients

1 heaping tablespoon (10 grams) ground flaxseed meal
2¹/₂ tablespoons (37.5 grams) water
1 cup (227 grams) Earth Balance Soy-Free Buttery spread, cold
¹/₄ teaspoon (1.5 grams) salt
³/₄ cup (150 grams) white granulated sugar
¹/₂ cup (60 grams) white confectioners' sugar, or powdered sugar
2 teaspoons (8 grams) pure vanilla extract
3 cups (375–390 grams) all-purpose flour, plus extra for rolling
1 teaspoon (5 grams) aluminum-free baking powder
1 tablespoon (7.5 grams) cornstarch

Instructions

1. Mix ground flaxseed and water in a small bowl and set aside to coagulate, about 5 minutes. Or use another egg replacement.
2. Cream cold buttery spread, salt, and sugars in a stand mixer with paddle attachment for 30 seconds.
3. Add vanilla and egg replacement on medium speed just until incorporated.
4. Mix dry ingredients (flour, baking powder, and cornstarch) in a separate bowl with a whisk, or sift dry ingredients together. Then, add dry ingredients to wet ingredients.
5. Mix on low speed. The dough will start pulling off the sides once it's combined. It will be a little sticky.

Continued on next page

6. Lay out a sheet of plastic wrap, place dough on top, and form it into a disc shape to allow dough to chill quicker. Wrap and place in refrigerator for at least 30 minutes for dough to firm up a little to prevent spreading.

7. Preheat oven to 350°F. Line a cookie sheet with parchment paper or prepare to lay dough on a bare restaurant-grade aluminum baking sheet.

8. Flour your surface. To get even dough, roll slowly up, down, and then to the sides. Roll dough out to ¼-inch thick minimum and cut your cookies into desired shapes.

9. Place cookies about 2 inches apart on a sheet, and bake for 10 to 11 minutes, or until the cookie puffs up and the center looks matte.

10. Once baked, let sit for 1 minute on the cookie sheet to firm up. Then transfer to a cooling rack.

MASTER TIPS

The heaping tablespoon of flaxseed will create a thicker egg replacement in the cookies. This will help the dough bind better.

The refrigeration step is crucial to keep your sharp edges.

If you're just looking for dairy-free, go ahead and use a regular large egg.

Gluten-Free Chocolate Cookies

Makes 24 large cookies

People who are gluten intolerant can get ready for chocolate sugar cookies! And I'm ready to deliver a treat! These are so delicious, they remind me of a brownie. The warm smell of chocolate baking in a brown-sugar cookie will fill your kitchen as you wait impatiently for these. There are so many health restrictions, and I want everyone to be able to indulge in a delicious treat.

Ingredients

1 cup (227 grams) unsalted butter, softened
1/2 teaspoon (3 grams) salt
1/2 cup (100 grams) granulated sugar
1/2 cup (110 grams) firmly packed light brown sugar
1 large egg (50 grams)
2 teaspoons (8 grams) pure vanilla extract
2 1/4 cups (325 grams) Bob's Red Mill 1-to-1 Baking Flour, plus extra for rolling
1/2 cup (43 grams) unsweetened gluten-free cocoa powder

Instructions

1. Cream butter and salt together in a stand mixer on medium speed for 30 seconds to incorporate the salt to the butter.

2. Add in sugars and mix for 1 minute on medium speed.

3. Add in egg and vanilla and mix together for 30 more seconds or just until incorporated.

4. Mix dry ingredients (gluten-free flour and cocoa powder) in a separate bowl. Sift if you'd like. I use a whisk to blend the dry ingredients together.

5. Add dry ingredients to your wet ingredients. Mix until a dough forms and pulls away from the sides of the bowl. It will be a little sticky.

6. Remove dough from bowl, wrap in plastic, and place in fridge for at least 1 hour. I find that a little extra chill time helps the gluten-free cookies keep their shape. If you flatten the dough, it gets colder quickly.

Continued on next page

7. Preheat oven to 375°F.

8. Flour your surface with gluten-free flour and roll dough out to ¼-inch thick. Cut your cookies into desired shapes.

9. Place about 2 inches apart on an aluminum restaurant-grade baking sheet or nonstick baking sheet lined with parchment paper bake for 6 to 7 minutes, or until the cookie puffs up and it's matte on the top. These will bake quickly, so keep an eye out. Add an extra minute for thicker cookies.

10. Once baked, let sit for a couple minutes on the cookie sheet to firm up. They will crumble if you don't give them a minute. Then, transfer to a cooling rack so they can cool completely.

MASTER TIPS

I have tried many 1-to-1 flours for baking, and while there are others that work great, I prefer Bob's Red Mill for my cookies. It has a very mild flavor that doesn't alter the taste much from an all-purpose flour cookie. The dough will be sticky—that's normal.

I use Hershey's unsweetened cocoa powder for my chocolate cookies.

Freeze the baked cookies overnight and pull them out when ready to frost for an extra soft bite.

Make sure not to overbake because they will become dry and hard. They can even be a little underbaked for a softer bite.

Sugar-Free Cut-Out Cookies

Makes 24 large cookies

One of my good friends is sugar free, and I deeply admire the dedication he has to his health. I know that many people face issues with sugar in their diets or their children can't have sugar. One of my mantras is "baking memories," which I want the whole family to do together. I have worked hard to get this right. I remember my sister telling me, "Don't compare it to your sugar cookie because it will never be that. Make a new flavor of cookie and just make it taste good."

Date sugar—what in the world?! It really works to add sweetness, but it is a little dry, so reducing the amount of flour is crucial. I added monk fruit sweetener to give it a little sugary taste. It's tricky because nothing will ever compare to the taste of pure granulated sugar, but I hope you'll give this a try.

Ingredients

1 cup (227 grams) unsalted butter, softened
1/2 teaspoon (3 grams) salt
1 cup (136 grams) dried date sugar
1/4 cup (50 grams) monk fruit sweetener
1 large egg (50 grams)
2 teaspoons (8 grams) vanilla extract
2 cups (265 grams) all-purpose flour
1/2 teaspoon (2.5 grams) aluminum-free baking powder

Instructions

1. Cream butter and salt together in a stand mixer with paddle attached for 30 seconds to mix the salt in.
2. Add in date sugar and monk fruit sweetener to the mixer, and mix on medium speed for about 30 seconds to 1 minute.
3. Add in egg and vanilla, and mix until creamy for 30 more seconds.
4. Mix dry ingredients (flour and baking powder) in a separate bowl. Sift if desired. I use a whisk to blend the dry ingredients together.

Continued on page 117

5. Add dry ingredients to your wet ingredients. Mix until a dough forms and it pulls away from the sides of the bowl.

6. Remove dough, wrap in plastic, and place in fridge for 30 minutes. If you flatten the dough into a disc shape, it gets colder quickly. This will allow your dough to firm up a bit for rolling and getting sharp edges.

7. Preheat oven to 350°F.

8. Flour your surface and roll dough out to ¼-inch thick. Cut your cookies into desired shapes.

9. Place about 2 inches apart on an aluminum restaurant-grade baking sheet or nonstick baking sheet lined with parchment paper and bake for 9 to 11 minutes, or just until the cookie puffs up and the center is matte. Keep an eye on them.

10. Once baked, let sit for 1 minute on the cookie sheet to firm up.

11. Transfer to a cooling rack so they can cool completely.

MASTER TIP

We are baking these lower and slower. The cookies brown faster with the dried date sugar. The dried date powder adds sweetness that doesn't taste like chemicals, taste artificial, or carry a funny taste, but . . . it also dries things out. I used Lakanto brand monk fruit sweetener because years ago I was given a bag and it's the only brand I've worked with. You can add an extra yolk for moisture if you need it.

Buttercream Basics

Keep these tips and tricks in mind to have the best luck with the buttercream recipes in this book!

- Use a 2-pound bag of powdered sugar and simply add in the extra 1½ cups to make 9 cups total.

- I like my buttercream for piping to be nice and smooth. You will see in the directions that I only mix for a minute or two. Overmixing causes the buttercream to become a bit grainy with tiny air bubbles. We want a nice and smooth consistency. If you see any air bubbles, you can beat them out with a rubber spatula by smacking it back and forth against the side of your mixing bowl.

- You can still add your food colorings after mixing; this will not ruin the buttercream. I like to add food coloring in small batches, so I mix a cup or two at a time. Find what works best for you.

- Shortening gives the buttercream a smoother texture, which is ideal for piping flowers. If you use a vegetable shortening, I suggest Crisco. Make sure it's fresh and not sitting in the back of your cupboard; shortening gets rancid over time and develops a greasy, yucky taste. We don't want yucky anywhere near these delicious cookies! Fresh is best. You can

use a shortening that you prefer. I've also included an all-butter option if you want to skip it, though.

- The weather is a huge factor. When it's hot, you might need a tablespoon less milk, but when it's cold, you may need an extra tablespoon. After you make this once, you will figure out how much cream or milk works with your climate. The temperature of your house and humidity of where you live will determine how much milk to add. Start with the minimum and slowly add more to find what works best for you.

- I treat frosted cookies like cupcakes and don't stack them until the last minute. After piping your buttercream, allow 8 to 12 hours to dry the crust before stacking—24 hours, if you can wait that long, will make it even stronger. Store finished cookies in an airtight container on the counter; no need to refrigerate. You can freeze frosted cookies for 2 weeks, but I don't recommend more freezing time because it will change the texture of the buttercream.

- Store unused buttercream in refrigerator, then let buttercream come to room temperature on counter before frosting. It will be solid. I don't recommend freezing the buttercream itself. Instead, make it a day or two before you need to frost your cookies. If you absolutely have to freeze your buttercream, you can freeze in an airtight container for 3 months, let it defrost in the refrigerator, and then whip for a minute when dethawed.

- Try adding ¼ cup freeze-dried raspberries that have been crushed in the food processer to your buttercream. Another delicious add-in is ¼ cup crushed Oreos. Both will change the color of the buttercream but will still make beautiful bases to pipe on.

MASTER TIP

I always use fresh shortening because it develops a strange taste if it is sitting in the pantry for long. Don't overwhip because the shortening and butter get grainy after whipping too long. I use any kind of powdered sugar that the grocery store is carrying. Safeway brand seems to work great. C & H is a great one, as well. If you use heavy cream, you will have to add extra powdered sugar because heavy cream is so thick.

Crusting American Buttercream

Makes about 6 cups

For this recipe, we're going to cut the butter with vegetable-based shortening to form a crust—the crust will be strong, but remember, your cookies' designs can still be smashed if a lot of pressure is applied. The crust will help so that the design doesn't smear, too. The shortening also helps give it a smoother texture, which is great for piping cookies. They will crust over enough to gently stack. This buttercream is a little sweet, but the powdered sugar makes a strong crust, which pairs nicely with the cookies in this book because they're purposely not too sweet. It's a perfect balance! Typically, for a buttercream recipe, you would mix until light and fluffy—not this recipe. You want the buttercream to be nice and smooth, so you will mix for only a minute or two.

Ingredients

1 cup (227 grams) unsalted butter, softened
1 cup (184 grams) Crisco vegetable shortening
½ teaspoon (3 grams) salt
2 teaspoons (8 grams) pure vanilla extract
9 cups (1080 grams) confectioners' powdered sugar (white powdered sugar)
5–6 tablespoons (75–90 grams) milk or heavy cream

Instructions

1. Cream your butter, shortening, and salt in a stand mixer on medium speed for 2 minutes. Both must be at room temperature to prevent clumping.

2. Once creamed, add your vanilla. Mix again for 1 minute.

3. Sift your powdered sugar to make sure there are no clumps and add it in.

4. Place a towel over your mixer to prevent a powdered sugar storm.

5. Once mixed, add in your milk, starting with 5 tablespoons. You can always add more, but you can't take it out. Continue to add more than the recipe states if it's too thick. Remember, temperature and humidity factor in. If you find it's too soft, add in ¼ cup extra powdered sugar to thicken it up. Be careful because it will begin to taste like straight powdered sugar if you add too much.

6. Mix until smooth, about 1 minute on medium to high speed. Be sure not to overwhip your buttercream. DON'T panic! You won't ruin it if it whips longer. Store unused buttercream in an airtight container in the fridge for up to 2 weeks.

All-Butter American Buttercream

Makes about 6 cups

I love the all-butter option; it's amazingly delicious. For anyone who dislikes the idea of short-ening in their buttercream, this one's for you. This will form a thin crust because of the amount of powdered sugar.

Ingredients

2 cups (454 grams) unsalted butter, softened
1/2 teaspoon (3 grams) salt
2 teaspoons (8 grams) pure vanilla extract
9 cups (1080 grams) confectioners' powdered sugar (white powdered sugar)
5–6 tablespoons (75–90 grams) 2% or whole milk

Instructions

1. Cream your butter and salt in a stand mixer on medium speed for 2 minutes.

2. Once creamed, add your vanilla. Mix again for a minute.

3. Scrape down sides and mix again for 30 seconds.

4. Sift your powdered sugar to make sure there are no clumps and add it in. Place a towel over your mixer to prevent a powdered-sugar storm.

5. Once mixed, add in your milk, starting with 5 tablespoons. You can always add more, but you can't take it out. Continue to add more than the recipe states if it's too thick. Remember, temperature and humidity factor in. If you find it's too soft, add in ¼ cup extra powdered sugar to thicken it up. Be careful because it will begin to taste like straight powdered sugar if you add too much.

6. Mix until smooth, about 1 minute on medium to high speed. Be sure not to overwhip your buttercream. DON'T panic! You won't ruin it if it whips longer. Store unused buttercream in an airtight container in the fridge for up to 1 week or freeze for up to 3 months.

MASTER TIP

If you have extra buttercream, you can freeze it in an airtight container for 3 months. Let it defrost in the refrigerator and then whip for 1 minute when dethawed. You can use heavy cream, but you will need quite a bit more to reach a piping consistency because heavy cream is so thick.

Sugar-Free Buttercream

Makes about 3 cups

This pairs perfectly with my sugar-free cookies. The sweetness of this buttercream balances out the cookie nicely. I am really excited to have an alternative cookie that is sugar free. I ate so many sugar-free substitutes to find the right one for you, and I think this is a great option. I really like the consistency that this buttercream offers. I hope you enjoy it.

Ingredients

1 cup (227 grams) unsalted butter, softened
¼ teaspoon (1.5 grams) salt
1 teaspoon (4 grams) pure vanilla extract
4½ cups (540 grams) powdered monkfruit sweetener
2–3 tablespoons (30–45 grams) 2% milk

Instructions

1. Cream your butter and salt in a stand mixer on medium speed for 2 minutes.
2. Once creamed, add your vanilla. Mix again for 1 minute.
3. Scrape down sides and mix again for 30 seconds.
4. Sift your monkfruit powdered sugar to make sure there are no clumps and add it in. Place a towel over your mixer to prevent a powdered-sugar storm.
5. Once mixed, add in your milk, starting with 2 tablespoons. You can always add more, but you can't take it out. Continue to add more milk than the recipe states if it's too thick. Remember, temperature and humidity factor in. If you find it's too soft, add in ¼ cup extra powdered monkfruit sweetener to thicken it up. Be careful because it will begin to taste like straight powdered monkfruit sweetener if you add too much.
6. Mix until smooth, about 1 minute on medium to high speed. Be sure not to overwhip your buttercream. DON'T panic! You won't ruin it if it whips longer. Store unused buttercream in an airtight container in the fridge for up to 1 week or freeze for up to 3 months.

MASTER TIP

If you're sugar free, then you're used to the taste of monkfruit sweetener—if not, it has a different aftertaste so be ready for that. I use Lakanto Brand monkfruit sweetener.

Vegan Buttercream

Makes about 3 cups

I've tried this with many different butter substitutions, but I always fall back on using Earth Balance Soy-Free Buttery Spread. You can use all shortening if you'd like.

Ingredients

1/2 cup (113.5 grams) Earth Balance Soy-Free Buttery Spread, cold
1/4 teaspoon (1.5 grams) salt
1/2 cup (92 grams) Crisco vegetable shortening
1 teaspoon (4 grams) vanilla extract
4 1/2 cups (540 grams) confectioners' powdered sugar
1–2 tablespoons (15 to 30 grams) almond milk (or more)

Instructions

1. Cream your spread and salt in a stand mixer on medium speed for 2 minutes.

2. Add in shortening and vanilla, mix until completely incorporated, about 1 minute.

3. Scrape down sides and mix again for 30 seconds.

4. Sift your powdered sugar to make sure there are no clumps and add it in. Place a towel over your mixer to prevent a powdered-sugar storm.

5. Once mixed, add in your almond milk, starting with 1 tablespoon. You can always add more, but you can't take it out. Continue to add more than the recipe states if it's too thick by adding 1 tablespoon extra at a time. Remember, temperature and humidity factor in. If you find it's too soft, add in ¼ cup extra powdered sugar to thicken it up. Be careful because it will begin to taste like straight powdered sugar if you add too much.

6. Mix until smooth, about 1 minute on medium to high speed. Be sure not to overwhip your buttercream. DON'T panic! You won't ruin it if it whips longer. Store unused buttercream in an airtight container in the fridge for up to 1 week or freeze for up to 3 months.

MASTER TIP

Add in vanilla almond milk for a little extra sweetness. Add in ¼ cup freeze-dried raspberries that have been pulsed in the food processor for a delicious treat.

Flooding Buttercream

Makes about 3 cups

This is technical; it's not easy. It may take you a handful of tries in your own kitchen to get the consistency that's right for you. Temperature outside and the warmth of your kitchen can determine how much cream you'll need. Heating in very short, small bursts and then stirring is crucial to getting the flood consistency right. I heat in the microwave for 4- to 5-second increments. If you overheat, the butter will melt and separate, and the buttercream will also run right off the cookie. If you don't heat it enough, you won't get a flat, smooth surface. It's tricky, but you can do it! I have found that heavy cream makes a thicker and flatter surface with fewer ripples.

The trick is to get the amount of heavy cream and heat right. If you're going to build a dam for the cookies and then fill, I suggest using a little thicker dam and then continuing to thin and heat for flooding consistency. This is not like royal icing where there is a timed consistency. This recipe is a great base to start. You may need to add more cream or heat longer, and that's okay. This is your starting place.

Keep in mind that buttercream will slightly change color when heated.

Ingredients

1 cup (227 grams) unsalted butter, softened
1/4 teaspoon (1.5 grams) salt
1 teaspoon (4 grams) vanilla extract
4 1/2 cups (540 grams) confectioners' powdered sugar (white powdered sugar)
5 tablespoons (75 grams) heavy cream plus more to reach flood consistency

Instructions

1. Cream your butter and salt in a stand mixer on medium speed for 2 minutes.

2. Once creamed, add your vanilla. Mix again for 1 minute.

3. Sift your powdered sugar to make sure there are no clumps and add it in. Place a towel over your mixer to prevent a powdered-sugar storm.

4. Once mixed, add in your heavy cream. Mix until smooth, about 1 minute on medium to high speed.

5. Take 1/2 cup of buttercream and put it into a microwave-safe bowl. Add in 3 tablespoons of heavy cream and stir.

6. Place bowl in microwave and heat for 15 seconds, stopping after each 5-second mark to stir. Don't heat for full 15 seconds at once; it will melt butter and separate. If you lift your spatula up and the buttercream that drizzles off isn't disappearing into the bowl with the rest of it, heat a little longer—5 seconds each time—and add in an extra teaspoon of cream at a time. You will find the perfect consistency with trial and error. When you are adding in more cream than recipe states, do so by teaspoon, not by tablespoon.

7. Place flood buttercream in a tipless piping bag or a squeeze bottle. Tie a knot at the top of the tipless bag to keep the buttercream from spilling out.

MASTER TIP

I find that a medium consistency works great on cookies. Add a dam by using thicker flood consistency. To thicken the flood buttercream, add in a little of your thick buttercream that you started with and stir until the lumps disappear.

Cream Cheese Frosting

Makes about 5 cups

Cream cheese frosting is delicious. This is a little sweeter than you're probably used to because of the high amount of powdered confectioners' sugar used to help the frosting form a thin crust.

Ingredients

1/2 cup (113.5 grams) unsalted butter, softened
1/2 teaspoon (3 grams) salt
1/2 cup (92 grams) Crisco vegetable shortening
1/2 cup (120 grams or 4 ounces) cream cheese, softened
2 teaspoons (8 grams) pure vanilla extract
7 1/2 cups (900 grams) or 1 (2-pound) bag of confectioners' powdered sugar
5–7 tablespoons (75–105 grams) 2 % milk

Instructions

1. Cream butter and salt in a stand mixer on medium speed for 1 minute.

2. Add in shortening and cream cheese and mix on medium speed for 2 minutes to lighten the color of the butter and cream everything together.

3. Scrape down the sides, add in vanilla extract, and mix again for 30 seconds.

4. Sift your powdered sugar to make sure there are no clumps and add it in. Add in 3 of the tablespoons of milk. Place a towel over your mixer to prevent a powdered-sugar storm.

5. Once mixed, add the other 2 tablespoons of milk. Mix for 10 seconds to see if you need more. Consistency should be thick like peanut butter. Add in more milk, 1 tablespoon at a time, to get to 7 tablespoons total if your buttercream seems too pasty and thick. You can always add more, but you can't take it out, so add in a little at a time. Continue to add more than the recipe states if it's still too thick by adding 1 tablespoon extra at a time. Remember, temperature and humidity factor in. If you find it's too soft, add in 1/4 cup extra powdered sugar to thicken it up. Be careful because it will begin to taste like straight powdered sugar if you add too much. If you're piping flowers, you'll want it thicker, and if you're piping through a small hole, you will want it to be thinner.

Continued on next page

6. Mix until smooth, about 1 minute on medium to high speed. Be sure not to overwhip your buttercream. This can get grainy if its overmixed; we want a smooth consistency for piping. If there are air bubbles, beat them out with a rubber spatula by hand—smack the buttercream back and forth in the bowl to press out the air.

7. Store unused buttercream in an airtight container in the fridge for up to 1 week or freeze for up to 3 months.

MASTER TIP

Piped cookies should be stored on the counter in an airtight container for 24 hours or in the fridge for 3 days, also in airtight container, to prevent cookies from drying out in the refrigerator. Frosted cookies can be frozen for 2 weeks. If you're looking for a longer shelf life, use the Crusting American Buttercream on page 121.

Chocolate Cream Cheese Frosting

Makes about 5 cups

I love a good chocolate cream cheese frosting; this one forms a thin crust and it's so delicious with its milk chocolate flavor. It's great for cookie cakes and for any cookie with brown or black frosting. If you add black food coloring to chocolate frosting, it colors much deeper and won't leave your mouth black.

Use black velvet cocoa powder for a really dark chocolate frosting—just substitute chocolate powders. This frosting is sweet so it will balance out the sugar cookies, and the powdered sugar gives it a crust. Black velvet works best to make black buttercream by adding some black gel to the frosting. You can use all butter instead of shortening, but I think the shortening gives it a smoother consistency when piping and helps with that crust.

Ingredients

$^1/_2$ cup (113.5 grams) unsalted butter, softened
$^1/_2$ teaspoon (3 grams) salt
$^1/_2$ cup (92 grams) Crisco vegetable shortening
4 ounces (120 grams) cream cheese, softened
$^2/_3$ cup (50 grams) unsweetened cocoa powder
2 teaspoons (8 grams) pure vanilla extract
$7^1/_2$ cups (900 grams) or 1 (2-pound) bag of confectioners' powdered sugar
6–8 tablespoons (90–120 grams) 2% milk

Instructions

1. Cream butter and salt in a stand mixer on medium speed for 1 minute.

2. Add in shortening and cream cheese and mix on medium speed for 2 minutes to lighten the color of butter and cream everything in.

3. Scrape down sides, add in vanilla extract and cocoa powder, mix again for 30 seconds.

4. Sift your powdered sugar to make sure there are no clumps and add it in. Add in 3 of the tablespoons of milk. Place a towel over your mixer to prevent a powdered-sugar storm.

5. Once mixed, add the other 3 tablespoons of milk. Mix for 10 seconds to see if you need more. It should be thick, like peanut butter. Add in more milk, 1 tablespoon at a time, to get to 8 tablespoons total if you feel like the frosting is still too pasty. You can always add more, but you can't take it out. Continue to add more than the recipe states if it's too thick by adding 1 tablespoon

Continued on next page

extra at a time. Remember, temperature and humidity factor in. If you find it's too soft, add in ¼ cup extra powdered sugar to thicken it up. Be careful because it will begin to taste like straight powdered sugar if you add too much.

6. Mix until smooth—about 1 minute on medium to high speed. Be sure not to overwhip your buttercream. This can get grainy if its overmixed, and we want a smooth consistency for piping. Store unused buttercream in an airtight container in the fridge for up to a week or freeze for up to 3 months.

MASTER TIP

Use Hershey's brand unsweetened cocoa powder or any dutched cocoa powder for a deeper chocolate. If there are air bubbles, beat them out with a rubber spatula by hand—smack the buttercream back and forth in the bowl to press out the air.

Glaze

Makes about ⅔ cups

I am such a huge fan of glaze. You can use the glaze instead of flooding buttercream. This is a lot simpler than the flooding buttercream and just as delicious. I love how soft it keeps the cookies after they set up. The lemon juice helps balance out the sweetness of the powdered sugar. Sift powdered sugar after measuring to make sure there are no clumps in the glaze.

Ingredients

1 tablespoon (20.5 grams) corn syrup
2 tablespoons (30 grams) plus 2 teaspoons (10 grams) milk
1 teaspoon (4 grams) vanilla extract, clear is preferred
½ teaspoon (2.5 grams) freshly squeezed lemon juice
2¼ cups (270 grams) confectioners' powdered sugar, sifted

Instructions

1. Mix corn syrup, milk, and vanilla together in a medium glass bowl.
2. Add in lemon juice and powdered sugar and mix until combined with a rubber spatula. It will take a minute.
3. Cover with plastic wrap and let air bubbles surface.
4. Pour glaze into smaller bowls and color to desired shades.
5. Put into tipless piping bags and pipe on decorations as if you'd pipe flooding buttercream.
6. Use a toothpick to pop any air bubbles in the bowl or on the cookie if you see any.
7. Let glazed cookies set up in an airtight container 8 to 12 hours or overnight for a wonderfully delicious cookie.

MASTER TIP

Dip cookies instead of piping. The kids love to mix their own colors and decorate with sparkles. Substitute honey for the corn syrup if desired.

Winter

For to us a child is born, to us a son is given, and the government will be on his shoulders. And he will be called Wonderful Counselor, Mighty God, Everlasting Father, Prince of Peace. —Isaiah 9:6

Vintage Christmas

page 138

Gingerbread Cookies

page 146

Vintage Christmas

This cookie set reminds me of the Christmas tree ornaments my Grandma Loopie would place on her Christmas tree every year. Very careful, not to touch, I admired them from afar. (Maybe I even touched a few when the adults weren't looking.) I bet, if you close your eyes, you can picture what your grandparents' Christmas trees looked like, too. I wanted to bring that joy to life in these cookies. Use colors that bring back nostalgia for you.

From the kitchen
Ornament-, square-, and present-shaped cookies
Flood-consistency buttercream
Squeeze bottle or tipless bag
Scribe or toothpick

From the drawer
Tip 2
Red, light green, turquoise, pink, and white food coloring gel
Cinnamon imperials

Round Ornament with Holly Instructions

1. With your warmed flood-consistency buttercream, make a rectangular box in the center from one side to the other and fill back and forth. Use a toothpick to make small circular motions to settle the buttercream and make smooth edges. Work quickly before the buttercream starts to cool and set.

2. With your light green buttercream, add in little green holly leaves by adding a drop of color and sweeping it over to the right with three points, as pictured. Use your red and make three holly berries just to the left of each leaf cluster.

3. Turn cookie upside down, and with white, make a straight line and a circle for the cap of the ornament.

4. Turn cookie on its side and make a thin, curved rectangle with light green buttercream.

5. On the bottom, use turquoise buttercream to fill the bottom of the ornament, outlining and filling it in. Use toothpick to make sharp edges by pulling the buttercream to its point.

6. To finish this ornament, outline and fill remaining area at top of cookie, just under cap.

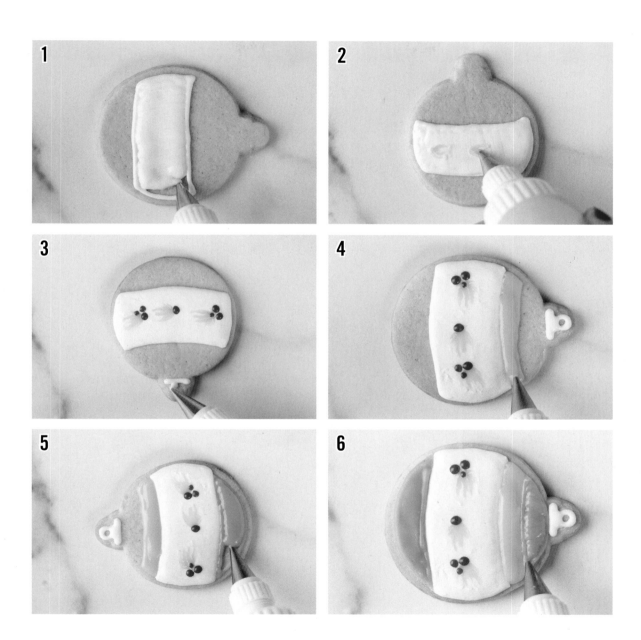

Continued on next page

Round Striped Ornament Instructions

1. Turn the cookie on its side. With white flood buttercream, make curved rectangular box in the middle, as pictured. Outline and fill.

2. Outline and fill a small space at the top of the ornament just under the cap. Make a small sliver of white on the bottom of the ornament.

3. Make a line of buttercream and a circle for the cap. They might bleed. If you wait 30 seconds to 1 minute between the line and the circle, they will remain intact.

4. In the first open space, fill with red flooding buttercream. In the bottom open space, fill with turquoise. Use a toothpick or scribe to flatten out any bumps by making small, quick, circular motions.

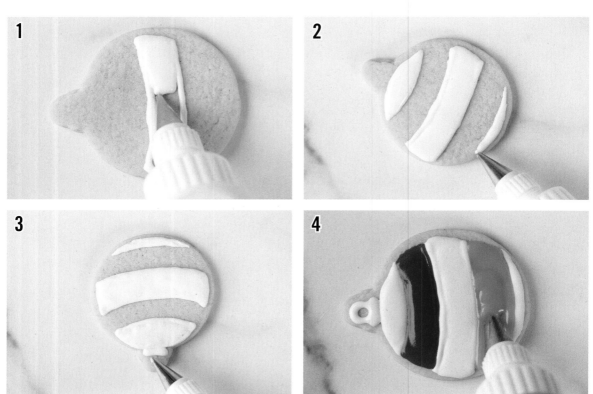

Teardrop Ornament Instructions

1. Use white flood consistency buttercream and split the ornament into three sections. First outline the far right and fill. Next go to the far left, outline, and fill. Follow the shape of the cookie, leaving the cap undecorated.

2. Now fill the middle section. Keep a tiny bit of space between the top points so the frosting doesn't flow together.

3. Wait 30 seconds and turn the cookie so the cap is toward you. Make a line, wait 1 minute or gently blow to create a little crust, and make the circle to complete the cap. Let dry for 10 minutes.

4. Turn the cookie right-side up and use turquoise buttercream to the left-side gap. You don't need to outline, just fill. Next, use pink buttercream to flood the last open space to the right.

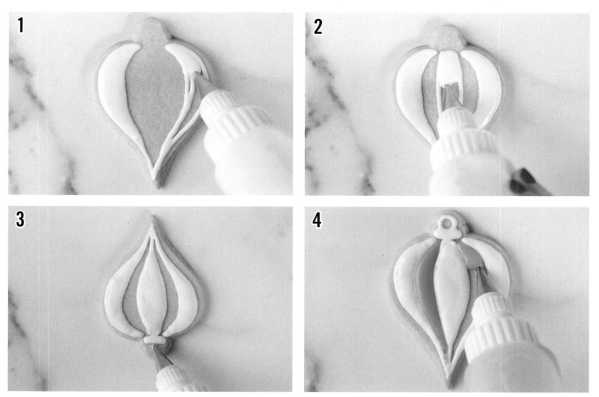

Continued on next page

Striped Present Instructions

1. Use red buttercream and make thick, diagonal lines by outlining and filling to get a thick look. Start in one corner.

2. Continue until there are 4 stripes that divide up the cookie. Let stripes dry for 5 minutes.

3. Take white buttercream and fill in the spaces of the cookie, creating thick stripes, and let set for another 5 minutes.

4. With red, draw thin lines diagonally down the cookie on top of the white.

5. With turquoise, make a bow in the corner. Draw a line horizontally and then vertically to cross, then make the bow in the center.

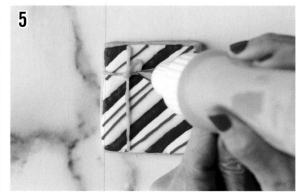

Red Present Instructions

1. Use red flood-consistency buttercream and outline the present.
2. Again, with the red, use lots of pressure when squeezing to quickly fill it up.
3. Make a ribbon with white. Make two vertical lines perpendicular in the middle of the cookie starting at the bottom to the top.
4. Again, using the white, make a small bow on top. I put a cinnamon imperial in the center of the bow, which is not pictured here.

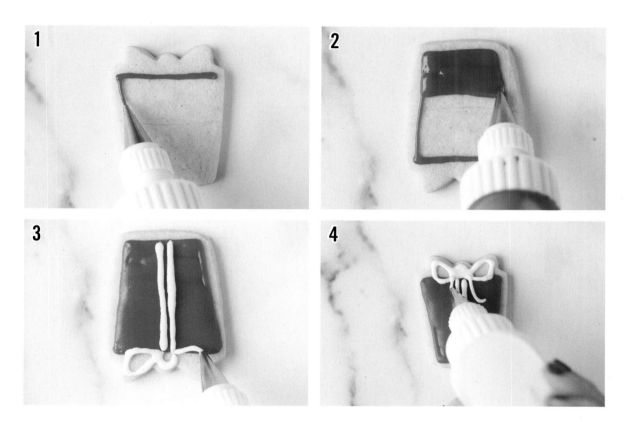

Continued on next page

Green Tree with Pom-Pom Garland Instructions

1. Use light green flood-consistency buttercream to outline and fill tree cookie quickly. Let set for 5 minutes.

2. With white flood buttercream, pipe a garland that drapes down from each section of branches to the lower opposite side. Let set for 5 minutes.

3. For the pom-poms, use two colors. Pipe first color and leave a space in between so you can add the alternating color.

4. Let first color set for 5 minutes and then pipe second color in between each open space to create a pom garland.

MASTER TIP

The flood consistency can be tricky and you will have to pipe quickly. Pipe a few bases and then move to the next step on a few cookies at a time, like an assembly line. It will make the wait time in between piping details very efficient. Mix up the colors to your liking.

Gingerbread Cookies

Gingerbread cookies are a Christmas classic. The smell alone brings me back to my childhood, baking for the holidays. They can be fully decorated or you can choose to just use some flood-consistency buttercream. The white makes a sophisticated contrast with the deep color of the gingerbread. The simplicity of this set is not only delicious but achievable for anyone. Use pastel colors to make the cookies pop. I can't believe I'm still rambling on—these cookies smell too delicious, get going!

From the kitchen

Gingerbread men-, stocking-, tree-, and
  snowflake-shaped cookies
Flood-consistency buttercream
Squeeze bottle or tipless bag
Scribe or toothpick
Cinnamon imperials

From the drawer

Tip 2
White food coloring gel
Cinnamon imperials
Silver dragees or silver sugar pearls

Gingerbread Man Instructions

1. Using white flood-consistency buttercream, outline the cookie, but don't pipe to the very edge. Pipe on a happy face.
2. Pipe rounded zigzags on wrists, feet, and on the head to make it look like a classic gingerbread man.
3. Finish off the cookie with cinnamon imperials for the buttons.

Gingerbread Woman Instructions

1. Take flood-consistency white buttercream and outline apron for the gingerbread woman.
2. Outline around the edge of the cookie, careful to not go to the very edge.
3. Make classic rounded zigzags for wrists, feet, and head.
4. Make the face and then use a toothpick to drag out the frosting for each eyelash.
5. Finish cookie with two cinnamon imperials for the buttons.

Continued on next page

Gingerbread Stocking Instructions

1. Outline the stocking with white flood buttercream and make a line to the cuff of the stocking.
2. Start in one corner and make small swirls and scrolls.
3. Continue with the swirls, connecting them together in some places for an elegant look.
4. Turn cookie to the side and fill the top of the stocking with buttercream; squeeze with an even amount of pressure all the way down.

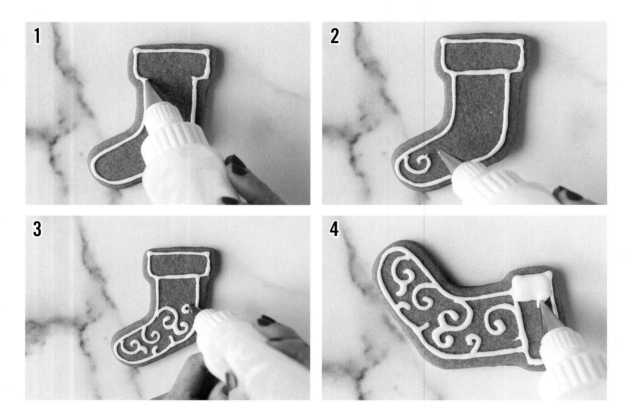

Gingerbread Snowflake Instructions

1. With white flood buttercream, pipe from one tip to the opposite. Make little dots of buttercream and pull it inwards to make the designs on the tips of the snowflake.
2. Continue to pipe and pull buttercream in until the snowflake is complete.
3. Add silver dragees or silver sugar pearls to each corner of the snowflake and one in the center.

Gingerbread Tree Instructions

1. Using the white flood buttercream, outline the tree cookie but don't go to the very edge.
2. Make lines going over and across to make boughs of the tree.
3. Place a silver dragee or silver sugar pearl at the top of the tree.

MASTER TIP

Use tweezers to strategically place the cinnamon imperials and the silver dragees. Use different colors of sugar pearls to add a little color to the cookie if you'd like. I love the simple and clean look to the white with a little accent of red and silver. Dress the gingerbread as you please; I love the apron because I feel in command when I'm wearing mine.

Santa Pants and Presents

page 152

Cookies for Santa
page 156

Santa Pants and Presents

These make me so happy! I was sitting there looking at the unfrosted present cookie, and I turned it upside down and just thought, "Hmmm, this looks like little feet.... Santa shoes ... Elf shoes! Ahhh, this is an idea!" Then, my sister and I were chatting over the cuteness of the pants cookies, and we thought it would be fun to put together an entire series of pants and feet! The possibilities had us beaming with excitement. Stay tuned for more!

From the kitchen	**From the drawer**
Present-shaped cookies	Tips 5, 18, and 2
Batch of buttercream	Red, black, white, yellow, brown, and green food coloring gel
	White nonpareils

Santa Pants Instructions

1. Turn the cookie so the bow is on the bottom. Using red buttercream and tip 5, outline the present but keep the bow unfrosted for now—those will be our shoes. Make a line for the seam of the inside of the pants, but don't go to the very top.

2. Start at the waist of the pants and pipe back a fourth with a steady stream of pressure, filling the pants. Go down each leg so it looks like they are separate legs.

3. Use white buttercream with tip 18 attached and pipe a fluffy border using a little bit of motion so it looks slightly wavy.

4. Using tip 2 and black buttercream, outline both parts of the bow and turn them into Santa's shoes. Pipe back and forth to fill it in.

MASTER TIPS

Mix the darker green to desired shade and scrape out the bowl, keeping a remnant in the bowl. Add in a cup of plain buttercream and mix, scraping the sides to mix in the green that was there. It will be a lovely shade of light green for your present. Make the presents any color you desire to make them your own.

To get a deeper shade of any color, wrap a bowl of frosting with plastic wrap and let it set overnight on the counter. Reds, blacks, and browns get richer and much deeper after sitting.

Use white for the elf pants design instead of white. I used yellow because it reminds me of Buddy the Elf.

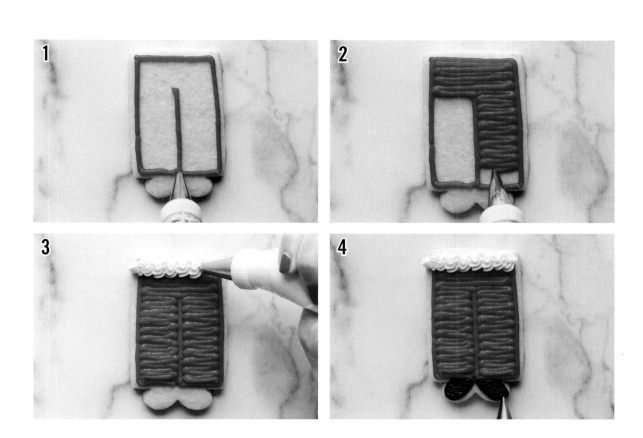

Continued on next page

Elf Pants Instructions

1. Turn cookie so bow is facing down. Use green buttercream with tip 5 attached. Outline the box but leave the bow unfrosted for now. Draw a seam for the pants up the middle and stop—don't go all the way to the top.

2. Using a back-and-forth motion and steady stream of buttercream, fill the elf pants. The seam will separate the pants for you so it looks like there are two legs.

3. Use tip 2 with yellow buttercream and pipe swirls up both outer edges of the pants for design.

4. Use black buttercream with tip 2 attached. Pipe where the bow would be and make the little shoes come to a point. Fill in back and forth until the shoes are solid black.

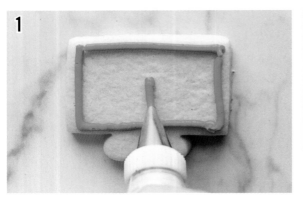

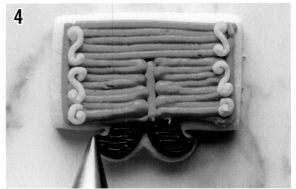

Present Instructions

1. Use tip 5 with light green buttercream and outline the present but keep the bow unfrosted. Pipe back and forth with a steady amount of pressure until the cookie is filled in.

2. Sprinkle white nonpareils on the present.

3. Use tip 2 and light brown buttercream. Pipe on ribbon to look like a few thicker strands of natural raffia. Make two to three layers to each part of the bow.

4. Next, using tip 5 and the same green used for the elf pants, make some dots of buttercream, gathered together to look like greenery or holly. Use red and tip 5 to make a few holly berries to complete the cookie.

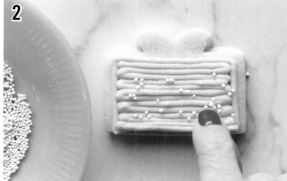

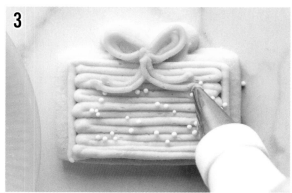

Cookies for Santa

I really wanted a cookie plate that would be fun to do with your whole family. Some of my fondest memories are getting cookies ready with my kids on Christmas Eve. I am using some simple, yet effective decorating techniques that will leave Santa wanting more. I am sure everyone will enjoy decorating these. Remember, dipping in sugar crystals is a beautiful and delicious way to hide any mistakes.

From the kitchen	From the drawer
Round and gingerbread man–shaped cookies Batch of buttercream	Tip 2 Red, black, white, brown, yellow, and green food coloring gel Tips 352, 48, 12, 5, and 2 Clear sugar crystals Cinnamon imperials

Santa Belly Instructions

1. Using red buttercream and the frozen buttercream technique on page 31, create a smooth base for Santa's Belly.
2. With tip 48 and black buttercream, pipe with the smooth end facing up and the ridged side down perpendicular to your cookie base.
3. Using yellow and tip 2, pipe on a square belt buckle.

Simple Holly Instructions

1. Use the frozen buttercream technique on page 31 to create a smooth base. Dip in clear sugar crystals or simply sprinkle them on once the buttercream has thawed a bit to make them stick on.

2. Use tip 352 and green buttercream to make three holly leaves in the top center. To make the first holly leaf, have the beak of the tip facing down as pictured. You should not be able to see the open part of the tip while piping. Angle the bag at 45° toward you. Start piping with a slight, gentle motion. Go forward and back ever so slightly to create a ripple, or bunching, to the leaves.

3. Add three cinnamon imperials to make the holly berries.

Continued on next page

Reindeer Instructions

1. Turn the gingerbread man on its head. Use tip 12 and light brown or tan buttercream. Hold the tip ¼ inch off the cookie base and position your bag straight up and down. This will make the buttercream flow flatter. Fill the bottom half for the face.

2. Make two ears where the gingerbread man's hands would be. These will be your reindeer's ears.

3. Dip the cookie straight into a plate of clear sugar crystals and gently press to fully coat. Don't smash.

4. With a darker shade of brown, use tip 5 and pipe on the horns. Making three to four points to the antlers on each side.

5. Next, use tip 2 and black buttercream and make small dots for the eyes.

6. Lastly, put a tiny dot of buttercream on where the nose will go and then place a red cinnamon imperial to make a bright red nose.

MASTER TIPS

Practice your holly on a plate or parchment paper to understand how to make leaves. The faster you pipe, the skinnier the leaf. Slower and more pressure will create a fuller leaf.

If you don't like cinnamon imperials, you can use red dots of buttercream with tip 5.

Use one small drop of brown to 1 cup buttercream to get a tan color. Use 6 to 7 drops (or more as needed) for a darker shade of brown. The more you add, the darker it will become.

Make a white buckle if you don't want to make a small amount of yellow for Santa's belt.

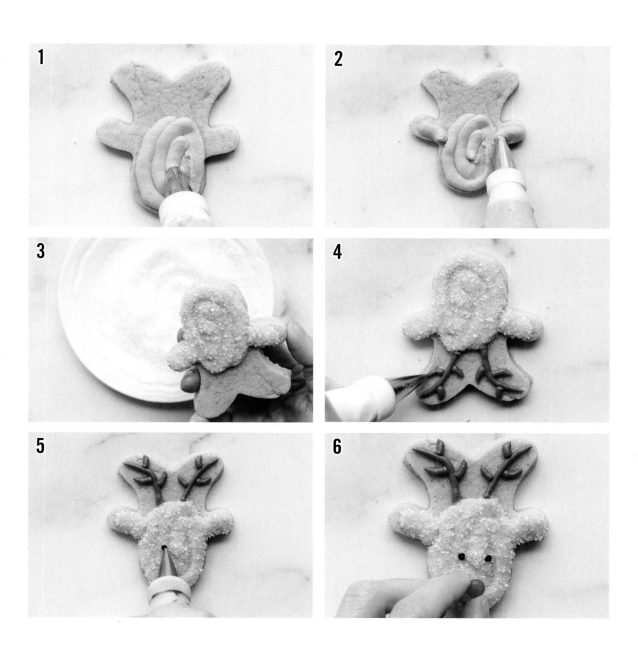

Peace and Joy Cookies
page 162

Sent with Love

page 167

Peace and Joy Cookies

These cookies remind me of a 1950s Christmas with the pink, silver, and red. If I had edible tinsel to throw on the buttercream trees, it would have fit perfectly. The trees have more of a ruffled look but not ribbon ruffles. It's more of an individual ruffle or "petal" for each branch. The white tree is so beautiful and clean, the sugar crystals just pop off.

The Poinsettia cookie is one of those designs I made years ago—it stuck and happily followed me. I made a pretty pink one for this set. The leaves are a little bunched to add texture.

From the kitchen

Tree- and round-shaped cookies

Batch of buttercream

From the drawer

Tips 366, 352, 104, and 5

Red, white, brown, pink, and moss green food coloring gel

Silver dragees

Red and pink sugar pearls

White nonpareils

Pink Poinsettia Instructions

1. Use tip 366 and pink buttercream. Hold piping bag about ¼ inch off the cookie base. Have beak of tip pointing down, as pictured. Start a little off center and keep space for the middle leaves. Squeeze a burst of buttercream and gently move in and out to create a ripple look of the leaves.

2. Make 6 leaves to create the bottom base of the poinsettia.

3. In the open space for the center, pipe smaller bursts for the smaller leaves. Pipe about 5 this time.

4. Add in silver dragees for the center of the poinsettia.

5. With tip 352 and moss green buttercream, pipe leaves in each open space around the poinsettia.

6. Gently move in and out with the piping bag to create the ripples in the green leaves as well.

Continued on next page

Ruffle Tree Instructions

1. Use tip 104 and moss green or white buttercream. Turn cookie upside down. Hold your piping bag at a 45-degree angle, the skinny end of the tip facing away from you and the wide end toward you, at the base of the cookie. Start piping in the bottom section of the tree. Pipe small individual petals for the first layer.

2. Pipe right under the first layer to create volume.

3. Move to the center of the cookie. These petals or branches will be longer and more ruffled. Squeeze a steady amount of pressure, pulling up and down to make each one.

4. For the top bough, create three large petals to close up the tree.

5. Turn cookie right-side up and, with tip 5 and brown buttercream, pipe back and forth to fill the trunk.

6. To complete the cookie, add white nonpareils and red and pink sugar pearls.

Continued on next page

Peace and Joy Instructions

1. Use the Freezer Frosting Method on page 31 for the base.
2. Use red buttercream and tip 5. Pipe the letters J O Y or P E A C E in the center of the cookie.
3. Pipe two dots before and after the JOY or PEACE.

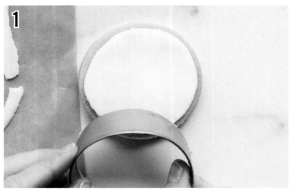

MASTER TIP

Practice the poinsettia leaves on a plate to get the ripple effect. Change the colors to fit any holiday color scheme.

Sent with Love

Valentine's Day is the day for love. These cute little cookies are so fun. Filling out Valentine's Day cards with my kids was always something I really looked forward to. Each kid picked out their own different cards. I loved the Hannah Montana stage Reese was in, then Nick loved Monsters, Inc., and Mikie loved Batman. Such a special time that goes by too fast. Personalize these with To- and From- on the envelope.

From the kitchen	**From the drawer**
Rectangle- and scalloped heart–shaped cookies	Tipless piping bags or a squeeze bottle
Batch of buttercream for flooding	Tip 2
	Scribe tool or toothpick
	Heart sprinkles
	White icing color and pink food coloring gel

Letter Instructions

1. Use a rectangle cookie and white flooding buttercream in a tipless bag or a squeeze bottle with a tip 2 attached. Pipe around the edges and fill all the way down the cookie.

2. Let dry for 5 minutes. Outline the cookie and make the fold for the envelope.

3. Place a heart sprinkle to seal the letter.

Continued on next page

Heart Instructions

1. Use pink flooding buttercream and pipe around the heart but don't go into the scalloped edges.
2. Squeeze the buttercream to fill in the cookie, working your way down. Use a steady stream of pressure.
3. Take a toothpick or scribe tool and swirl out those lines or any bumps.
4. Take white, thicker-consistency flood buttercream and make dots all the way around the cookie in the scallops.

Stitched Heart Instructions

1. Use pink flooding buttercream to outline and fill in the heart.
2. Use a toothpick or scribe to swirl out the bumps.
3. Take white flooding buttercream and pipe small lines around the outside of the pink to make stitching.

MASTER TIP

Mix in some red or purple hearts for Valentine's Day. Add some glitter or sprinkles to the edges or center of the hearts.

Dipped Hearts

page 171

Dipped Hearts

These were so fun to make with my boys. Even though it's "girly," they love me, and it makes me happy that they were willing to make them. You can see where Mikie had to add some turquoise color, which I absolutely love. Scalloped heart-shaped cookies would also be beautiful on these.

From the kitchen	**From the drawer**
Heart-shaped cookies	Red and turquoise food coloring gel
Batch of flooding buttercream	

Follow Dip Method on page 24.

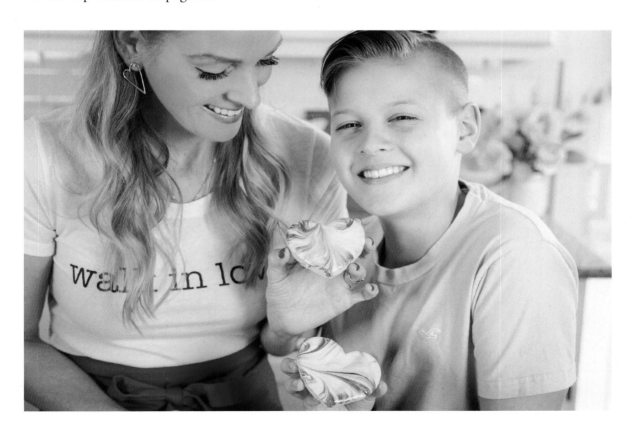

Spring

2 Corinthians 5:17 Therefor, if anyone is in Christ, the new
creation has come: The old has gone, the new is here!

Rainbows
page 176

Lucky Charms

page 178

Rainbows

The rainbow that comes after the storm is so powerful because it's a sign of hope. I am such a believer in spreading joy and hope. Somehow, through all the hard times in my life, God's truth and promises have never let me down. I choose to believe in his perfect plan and that hope is always on the horizon, just like a rainbow after a storm.

I turned the cookies green with green food coloring in the dough and added edible glitter straight onto the cookie for a sparkle and shine before I baked them. We have to add bling for St. Patrick's Day.

From the kitchen
Rainbow-shaped cookies
Batch of buttercream

From the drawer
Red, orange, yellow, green, blue, purple, and white food coloring
Gold confetti sprinkles
Gold edible glitter, optional
Tips 21 and 12

Instructions

1. Use the Multi-Colored Buttercream on page 28 and attach tip 21. Turn the rainbow cookie upside down so the clouds are facing upward. Pipe a stream of buttercream from one end to the other with the red, orange, and yellow colors coming through the buttercream.

2. Make the bottom part of the rainbow but rotate so colors green, blue, and purple are on the top this time. This will give you a full rainbow of colors.

3. With white buttercream and tip 12, pipe bursts of buttercream for the clouds and layer a few on the very top to make it look fluffy. Hold your piping bag straight up and down, squeeze until the buttercream billows out, and give it a little twist at the top to make the dollops flat and not look like Hershey's kisses.

4. Add gold confetti for Leprechaun gold.

MASTER TIP

Add ¼ teaspoon mint into the thick cookie dough for a nice, minty flavor that reminds me of a Shamrock Shake. Add mini chocolate chips or white chocolate shards to the dough. These are simple and fun for the whole family to enjoy.

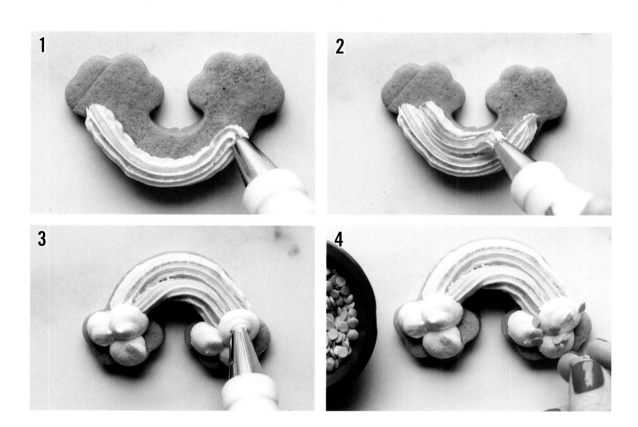

Lucky Charms

Lucky Charms were one of my absolute favorite cereals growing up. My sisters loved it, too. How fun to make little marshmallows out of buttercream to make them sweet and simple. Sometimes less is more.

From the kitchen
Round cookies
Batch of buttercream

From the drawer
Offset spatula
Tip 5 and 2
Green, blue, yellow, red, and pink food coloring

Heart Instructions

1. Use the Frozen Flat Technique on page 35 and offset spatula to smooth the surface, if needed.
2. With pink buttercream and tip 5 attached, pipe a small heart in the center.
3. Take the spatula and gently smooth the lines in the heart.

Hat Instructions

1. Use tip 2 and light green to pipe a small hat in the center of the cookie, outline, and fill it in.
2. With the offset spatula, smooth the hat so there are no lines.
3. Using a darker green and tip 2, pipe a lucky four-leaf clover on top.

Continued on next page

Balloon Instructions

1. Use tip 5 and red buttercream to pipe a red balloon in the center of the cookie on the flat white surface.
2. Use the spatula to flatten and lines to make it look like a marshmallow.

Moon Instructions

1. Using light blue buttercream and tip 5, pipe a moon in the center of the cookie.
2. Use the offset spatula to flatten lines and make the moon's nose prominent.

Rainbow Instructions

1. Use tip 2 and light blue buttercream to pipe the first part of the rainbow in the center of the cookie.
2. Follow with yellow and then pink in the center of the rainbow.

MASTER TIP

The freezer flat method is so simple, but you can just pipe on buttercream and simply smooth with your offset spatula. Make the rest of the Lucky Charms marshmallows for a really fun set.

Baskets and Bunny Butts

page 184

Easter Friends

page 188

Baskets and Bunny Butts

Who doesn't love a bunny butt cookie! I love the aerial view inside of these baskets. I always try to see things from different angles and perspectives, especially when I'm frosting cookies. Zhush these up with some egg sprinkles or easter-colored nonpareils, and you'll have darling cookies. Can we take a moment to think about the bags of Cadbury mini chocolate eggs that I have to hide from my kids to make sure I have them available for these?

From the kitchen

Bunny-, jelly bean- and round-shaped cookies

Batch of flooding buttercream

Batch of buttercream

From the drawer

Tipless piping bags or squeeze bottle with small round tip attached

Tips 2, 233, and 18

Scribe tool or toothpick

Pink, purple, turquoise, green, and white food coloring

Pastel nonpareils

Mini chocolate Cadbury eggs

Egg-shaped sprinkles (optional)

Sugar crystals

Bunny Butts Instructions

1. With the flood-consistency buttercream in a squeeze bottle with small round tip attached (I'm using a tip 2 but you can use a tipless piping bag), outline ears and fill in.

2. Then outline the head and fill in with firm pressure. Continue outlining and filling for the body.

3. Sprinkle some clear or pink sugar crystals on the bunny.

4. Using tip 18 and regular buttercream colored white, pipe a round dollop of buttercream and swirl it at the top so it looks like a cute, fluffy bunny tail.

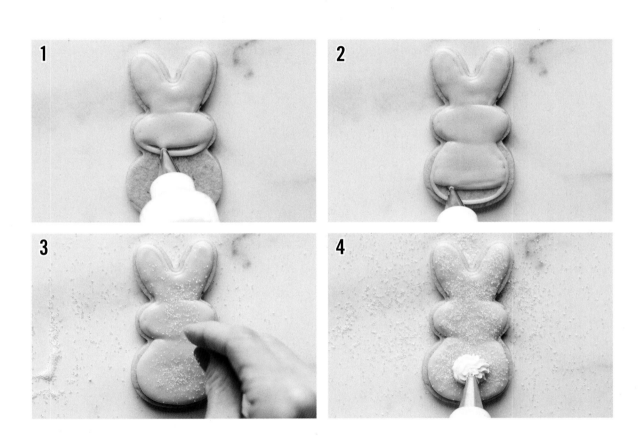

Continued on next page

Jelly Bean Instructions

1. Using purple flooding buttercream, outline and fill jelly bean cookie.
2. Take a scribe tool or toothpick and swirl around the edges if you need to work the buttercream closer to the edge.

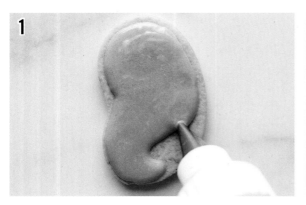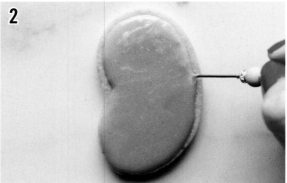

Baskets Instructions

1. Use regular white buttercream with tip 18 attached. Make small crisscross piping motions along the outer edge of the round cookie.
2. Pipe small, overlapping crisscross all the way around and close it. This is the basket rim.
3. With light green buttercream and tip 233, pipe the center of the basket, starting in the center and moving toward the outside.
4. Then create grass by holding the piping bag straight up and down about ¼ inch off of the green base we just created. Squeeze buttercream out and stop. Pull away, breaking the buttercream to make the grass.
5. Sprinkle with pastel nonpareils
6. Add in three eggs to complete the easter baskets.

MASTER TIP

Make birds' nests with tip 233. Add in actual jellybeans in place of the chocolate eggs, or add jelly beans in beside them. Change up the color of the grass in the baskets to pink, blue, or purple to look like Easter basket grass filler.

Easter Friends

I wanted to tie in a lamb for Easter and a design that is darling but simple. These little Easter friends are absolutely adorable and make my heart so happy! The little chick is sweet and happy, the bright yellow is like sunshine. My cousin Morgan has some amazing bunnies, and I love the ones with floppy ears—they are so beautiful. That was my inspiration for the floppy-eared bunnies in this set.

From the kitchen
Round-shaped cookies
Batch of buttercream

From the drawer
White, brown, yellow, orange, pink, and
   black food coloring gel
Tips 12, 352, and 2
White nonpareils
Parchment paper
Tapered offset spatula

Lamb Instructions

1. Use the Parchment Method on page 21 and white buttercream to start with a smooth, flat surface. Use tip 12 and hold your piping bag straight up and down, ¼ inch off of the cookie base, and start squeezing—don't move the piping bag, let the buttercream billow out the sides to create the first circle. Once the circle is the desired width, round off the bag instead of pulling straight up. This will break the buttercream and smooth the top so it doesn't look like a Hershey's kiss. Pipe those same dollops all around the border of the cookie for the lamb's wool.

2. Next, pipe more to fill the top and the bottom so it looks fluffy.

3. Dip lamb straight down into white nonpareils.

4. With black buttercream and tip 2, pipe the eyes on the lamb.

5. Next, with tip 2 and pink buttercream, pipe the nose in a heart shape.

6. Again, with the black, pipe the mouth of the lamb.

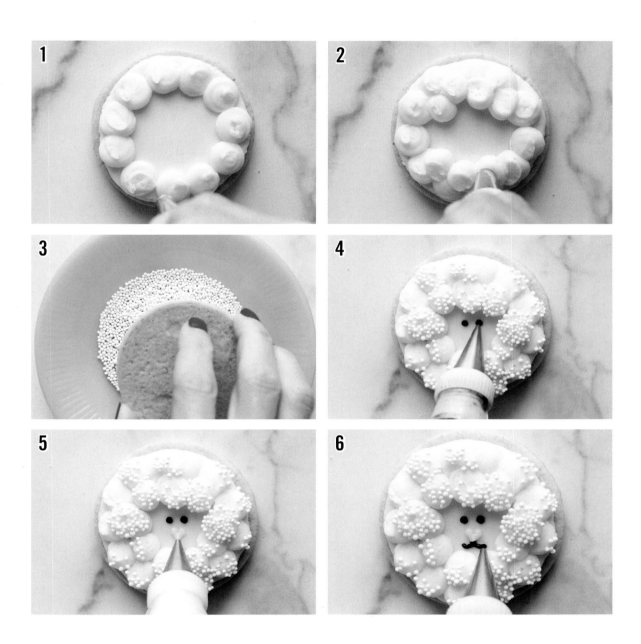

Continued on next page

Chick Instructions

1. Use the Parchment Method on page 21 with a yellow base. Take tip 352 and pipe some feathers. Hold the beak of the piping tip down to the base of the cookie, squeeze out buttercream with firm pressure, and pulse in and out to create ruffles in the feathers. Stop squeezing where you want the feather to end. Pipe a bunch (about 7 to 8 feathers). This is the top of the chick.

2. Next, turn the cookie to the side and pipe two feathers.

3. Do the same thing on the opposite side of the chick for the wings.

4. With black buttercream and tip 2, pipe small dots for the eyes.

5. Also using tip 2, but with orange buttercream, pipe a small V for the beak.

6. For the feet, use orange again, and pipe a little arrow shape for each one.

MASTER TIP

Make light brown bunnies—or even pink bunnies would be adorable. Change up the color of the chicks for a fun set; make them your own. You can dip the lamb in sugar crystals instead of the nonpareils, but I thought the nonpareils gave it a great texture.

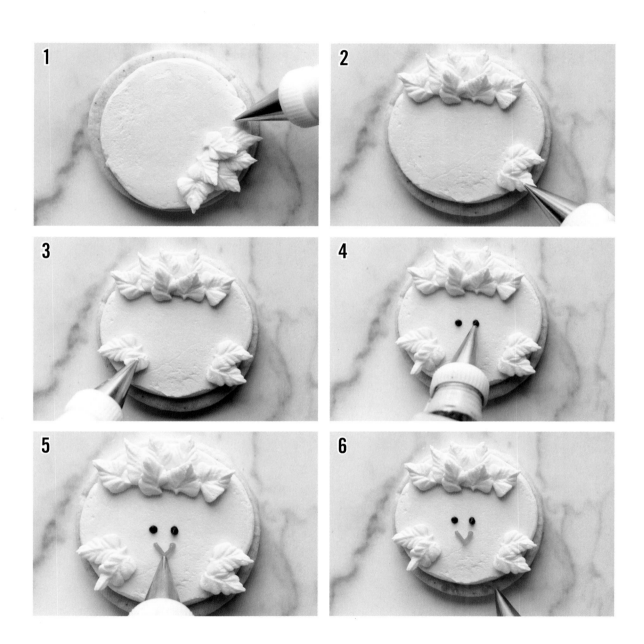

Continued on next page

Floppy-Eared Bunny Instructions

1. Use the Parchment Method on page 21 with brown buttercream. Take the same brown buttercream and attach tip 12. Hold your piping bag straight up and down, about ¼ inch off the base. Pipe the ears by starting at the top on the outside, pipe down, and come back up and stop. Do this for both sides of the cookie.

2. Use your tapered offset spatula and gently smooth the ears, blending the top of the ears down to the base so it looks like they are one with the face.

3. Next, make two dollops of buttercream in the center of the cookie for the cheeks. Roll the tip in a rounding motion to make a flat dollop. If you just stop squeezing and pull straight up, the buttercream will have a Hershey's kiss tip.

4. With tip 2 and pink buttercream, pipe a heart nose just above the cheeks.

5. With the black buttercream and tip 2, pipe tiny dots for the eyes.

6. Lastly, using black, pipe a cute little smile just under the cheeks.

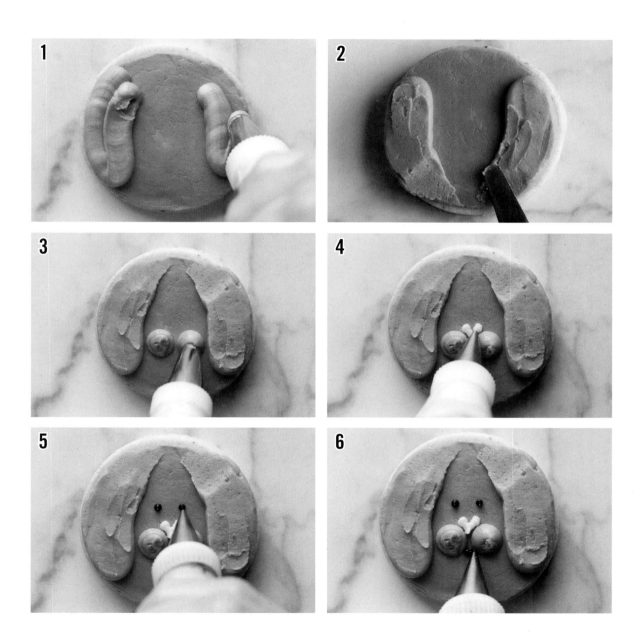

Summer

"Keep your face toward the sunshine and the shadows will fall behind you."
—Walt Whitman

Summer Beach

page 198

Houseplants
page 204

Summer Beach

Sitting with my toes in the sand next to the ocean is like Heaven on Earth. Don't forget your large-brimmed hat to shade the sun. These cookies take me right to the beach—aren't they fun?! My friend Liz of Inspired to Taste *created these cookies cutters and I had so much fun using them.*

It should go without saying, but read the full instructions and Master Tips before starting on this set!

From the kitchen	From the drawer
Hat-, bathing suit- and tote bag-shaped cookies Batch of flooding buttercream 1/2 batch of regular buttercream	Tipless piping bags Piping bags Couplers Scribe tool or toothpick Tip 5 and 104 Yellow, pink, tan, and white food coloring gel

Bathing Suit Instructions

1. With light pink buttercream in a tipless piping bag, outline the bathing suit and fill with flood-consistency buttercream, but don't frost the ruffled sleeves. The tipless piping bag should have a small hole for this, not too big but not tiny.

2. Use a scribe tool to swirl out any bumps in the buttercream.

3. With yellow flood-consistency buttercream in a tipless piping bag with small hole, make four to five dots in clusters, leaving a space in the center. These will be little yellow flowers.

4. Again, use the scribe tool and pull the yellow into the middle to create each petal.

5. Take white flood-consistency buttercream and make small dots in the center of each yellow flower.

6. With thick white flood-consistency buttercream (thick like peanut butter), pipe on a ruffle with a piping bag and tip 104 attached. Hold the piping bag at a slight angle with the wide end at the top of the cookie so the ruffle will have a thin edge.

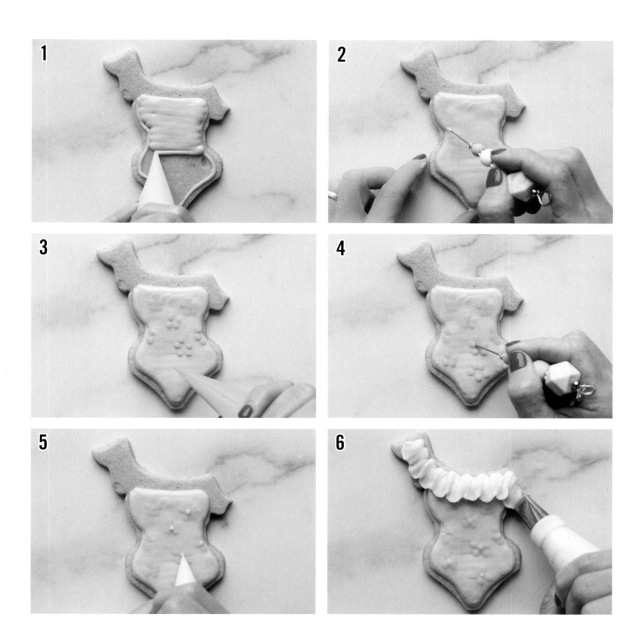

Continued on next page

Hat Instructions

1. Cut a small—but not tiny—hole in the bottom of a tipless piping bag. Use thicker consistency buttercream that won't melt into flood consistency. Start in the corner of the hat's brim. Pipe small crisscross patterns or offset X's.

2. Pipe all the way across the brim of the hat with that same pattern so it looks like a woven hat.

3. Then start piping the opposite way by tuning the hat to the other side with the bottom of the brim now facing up. Pipe the same crisscross pattern; we are following a pattern in which every line of crisscrosses will be facing the opposite direction to create texture.

4. For the third row, again rotate the cookie so the brim that was on the bottom is now facing away from you, at the top. Crisscross the row. Continue until the first part of the hat's brim is full.

5. Move to the empty part of the brim (the back of the floppy hat). Crisscross the same pattern to fill in, as pictured.

6. Then, pipe a line that will outline the brim of the hat.

7. Pipe the top of the hat in the same crisscross pattern, alternating directions for each row.

8. Use a piping bag with tip 5 attached and yellow thick-consistency flooding buttercream to pipe a ribbon that lined the top of the brim where the top meets. Make a little bow to finish the cookie.

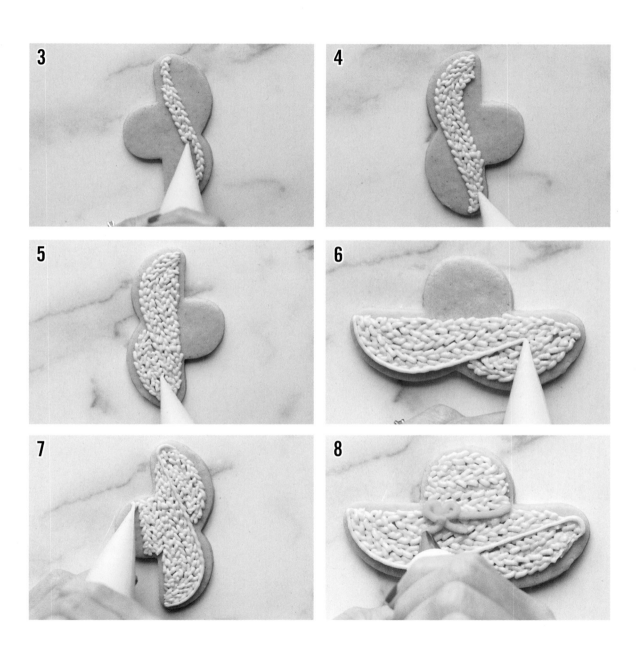

Continued on next page

Tote Instructions

1. Cut a small-to-medium hole in the bottom of a tipless piping bag—not tiny, but bigger than the hole we used for the hat. Use thicker-consistency buttercream that won't melt into flood consistency. With the tan, pipe crisscross patterns on each end of the bag. We're working our way inside to meet in the middle. For the second row, pipe the opposite direction, like we did with the hat.

2. Pipe up and down, coming further into the middle from the outside.

3. Stay with the same pattern, piping one direction in one row and then the opposite direction. Turn the cookie each time, crisscrossing.

4. Pipe one last crisscross line down the middle.

5. Outline the whole tote for definition.

6. With thick-consistency yellow in a piping bag with tip 5 attached, pipe a swirled handle to complete the summer tote.

MASTER TIP

For thicker flood buttercream, just don't add in the extra cream to thin it out. The crisscross patterns are simple, but it all comes together beautifully. Make the bathing suit and flowers any colors you wish.

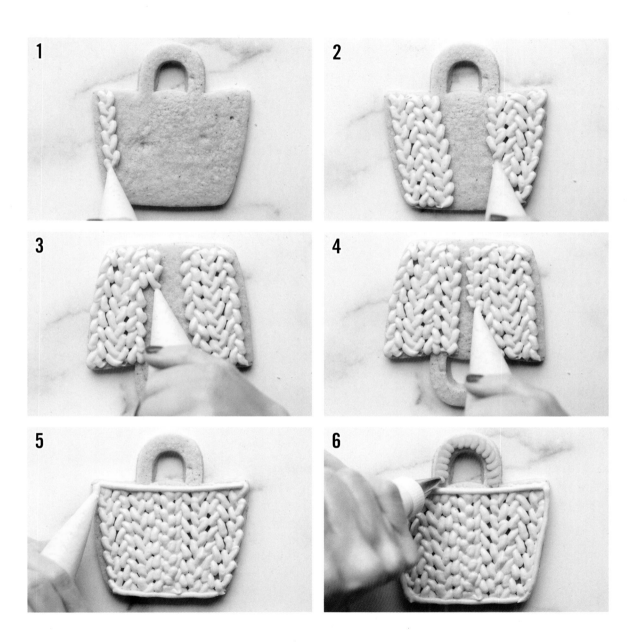

Houseplants

My sister got me hooked on houseplants; she's the queen plant lady. They liven up any space and give your home a cozy vibe for your guests. My plants thrived in the summer and fall but into the winter, they weren't doing so hot. I hope when the sun starts heating up the Pacific Northwest, my plants will be happy again. The good thing about these plant cookies is you get to eat them—no watering required!

From the kitchen
Rectangle- and round-shaped cookies
Batch of buttercream

From the drawer
Tips 2, 5, 102, 352, 10, and 47
Piping bags
Couplers
Offset spatula
Brown, orange, green, and white food coloring
White nonpareils
Tweezers

Pilea Peperomioides (Chinese Money Plant) Instructions

1. Use two parts orange and one part brown to get a terracotta color of buttercream. Attach piping tip 47, and pipe with the flat end of the tip face up. Pipe 4 rows that get longer as you go.

2. With an offset spatula, smooth the lines together.

3. Pipe a few dots of white buttercream on the brown. Use the spatula and smooth to get a rustic finish.

4. With tip 47 again, pipe one line to be the top of the pot.

5. Turn the cookie so the bottom is now facing away from you, and using tip 5 with green buttercream, pipe green stems that come from the pot.

6. Use tip 102 with the same green to pipe the leaves. Hold so the wide end touching the stem and the skinny end pointed away from you. This will give the leaf a thin tip. Pipe and round your wrist slightly to make a circle. (Practice on a plate before you start piping if you haven't used this tip before.) Use tip 5 to pipe on more stems between each one already piped to make the potted plant fuller. Reattach tip 102 and make more leaves to complete the plant.

Continued on next page

Bunny Ear Cactus Instructions

1. Follow steps and photos 1 through 4 of the Pilea Plant to make the terracotta pot. Turn the cookie so the pot is away from you. With green and tip 10, hold the piping bag about ¼ inch off the cookie and pipe an oblong or oval shape for the first couple of cacti.

2. Use a spatula to smooth the tops of each one.

3. Continue piping and smoothing to make a full cactus.

4. Use tweezers to place white nonpareils around for the spikes of the cactus.

Palm Plant Instructions

1. Follow steps and photos 1 through 4 of the Pilea Plant to make the terracotta pot. Use green buttercream and tip 5 to pipe three stems coming up from the pot.

2. Attach tip 352 to the green buttercream. Have the beak of the tip open so when you're squeezing, it's coming out from the open part of the tip. Hold the piping bag at a 90° angle, almost perpendicular with the cookie. Squeeze and pull the buttercream to create each leaf. Make a cluster on each stem.

3. Pipe until the stems are full of small palm leaves.

Continued on next page

Fern Instructions

1. Use white and tip 10 to pipe a pot shape at the bottom of the cookie. With an offset spatula, smooth the surface but keep the shape of the pot.

2. Hold the piping bag straight up and down for a flat flow of buttercream. Use the white again, and pipe one thick line on the top of the pot for the rim.

3. With the green and tip 2, start at the top of the fern and work your way down. If you squeeze the buttercream and pull toward the center for the left side of fern, and do the opposite for the right side, they will meet in the middle, as pictured.

4. Pipe ferns on the far right and far left of the pot. Pipe one larger one in the center, following the same instructions to pipe. Squeeze and slowly pull to the center of where the fern should be.

MASTER TIP

Practice piping leaves on a plate before moving to the cookie. Make the pots any color you desire. Add different shades of green to bring these to life.

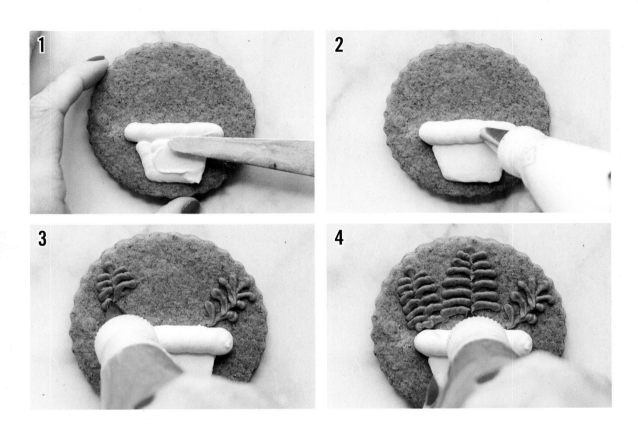

Fourth of July BBQ

page 212

Flower Child
page 218

Fourth of July BBQ

The Declaration of Independence of the United States was signed on July 4, 1776. The flag still stands for freedom, and I am proud to share these cookies with you. My friend Mary, of Emma's Sweets, made these cookie cutters, and I think they make the perfect set for the Fourth of July. The hot dogs look real, which is insane—it actually creeped us out for a second while we were shooting these cookies. They just look so real.

I really enjoy the BBQs and family gatherings held to celebrate America with my family and neighbors. These cookies fit in perfectly.

From the kitchen

Flag-, hot dog-, watermelon pop-, and firework-shaped cookies
Batch of buttercream
Batch of flooding buttercream

From the drawer

Tips 1A, 12, 18, and 2
Piping bags
Couplers
Tipless piping bags
Scribe tool or toothpick
Brown, red, green, blue, black, yellow, and white food coloring
White nonpareils

American Flag Instructions

1. Use tip 18 attached to a bag with blue buttercream and pipe a small rectangle of stars. Hold the piping bag straight up and down about ¼ inch off the cookie. Squeeze until the buttercream billows out and then stop squeezing and pull up your tip. Border and fill in the rectangle in the top left.

2. With white buttercream and tip 18 again, pipe stars on tip of the blue buttercream. Add as many as you can fit. I could only fit 12, but I think it looks great.

3. With red buttercream and tip 18, pipe the first stripe. Hold the tip right next to the blue rectangle at the top of the cookie. Start piping the buttercream so it billows out and then move the bag to the left and pull down to make a shell. Continue doing this to the end of the cookie where the fist stripe stops.

4. Next, use white buttercream and tip 18, and do the same shell piping for the white line.

5. Continue on, piping red, white, and red again.

6. The last row will be white and that completes our flag cookie.

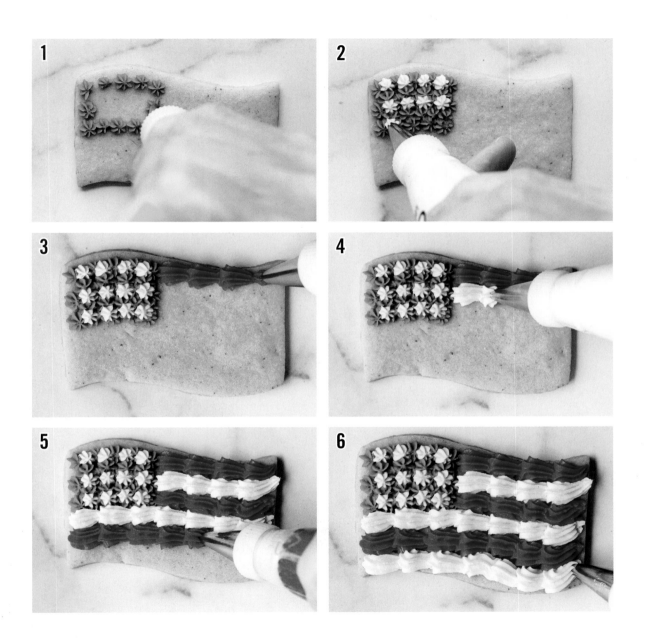

Continued on next page

Hot Dog Instructions

1. Use two parts brown and one part red to get a hot dog color. Use the two-toned painting technique on page 26 and brown food coloring to get the cooked look for the hotdog. Use tip 1A and hold the piping bag at an angle so it flows out like a tube of toothpaste. Pipe from one end of the hotdog to the other, right down the center. Stop piping and round it off with a twisting motion so the hot dog doesn't have a Hershey's kiss point to it.

2. Use light brown buttercream with tip 12 and pipe along the bottom of the hotdog for the bun.

3. Turn the cookie upside down and do the same thing at the other end.

4. With red buttercream and tip 5, pipe in a curved zigzag from one end of the hotdog to the other for the ketchup.

5. With yellow buttercream and tip 5, pipe the same pattern but staggered a little from the ketchup.

6. Sprinkle white nonpareils for onions on the hot dog.

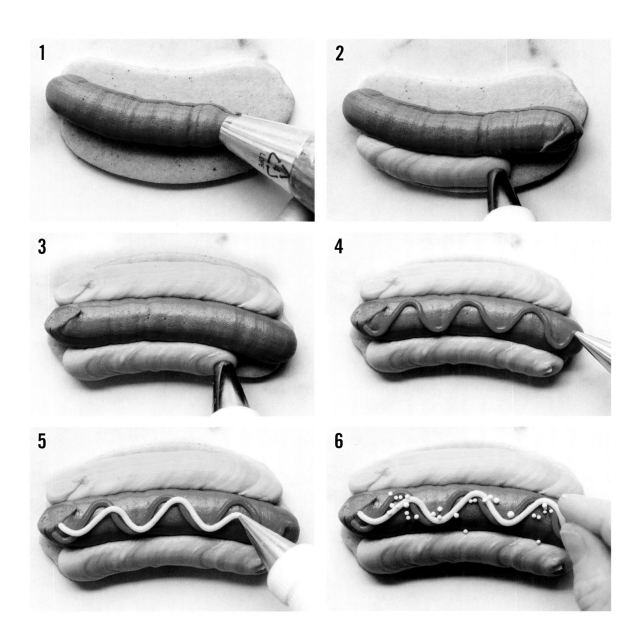

Continued on next page

Watermelon Pop Instructions

1. Use light brown and tip 12 to pipe the stick for the watermelon pop. If you hold the piping bag straight up and down, it makes for a wider and flatter flow of buttercream.

2. With tip 2 and dark green, pipe a thin line of buttercream for the outer rind. Use white buttercream and tip 2 to pipe another line just under that for the inner rind of the watermelon.

3. With pink flooding buttercream, flood the watermelon by outlining it and filling it in. Use a scribe or a toothpick and swirl out any bumps or lines.

4. Use black buttercream with tip 2 attached and pipe dots and bring them to a point for the seeds. Use the scribe tool to make the point of the seed look nice and sharp. Pull it toward you.

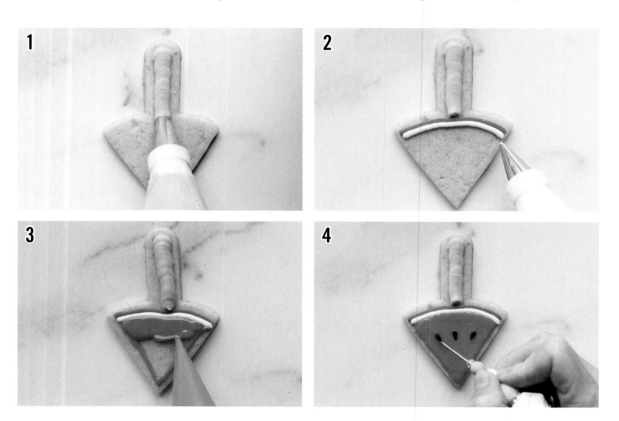

Firework Instructions

1. Use tip 18 and red buttercream. Start piping at one of the tips of the firework. Squeeze a dollop of buttercream and slowly pull on toward the middle, stopping once you reach the center.

2. Continue to fill the firework. Pipe and pull in with each part of the firework to meet in the center. Make some longer than others.

3. Hold the piping bag straight up and down and go to the very edge where there is some room and place little bursts of buttercream. Squeeze until the buttercream billows out and stop, then pull up. Make little bursts in any area that needs some firecracker.

4. Add white nonpareils to the center and sprinkle less as you go out to the edge of the cookie. Keep most of the sprinkles in the center.

MASTER TIP

Use sugar crystals in place of the nonpareils or add multicolored sprinkles to the fireworks. Make the fireworks hot pink or any color to bring more color to the cookie set.

Flower Child

I pray a lot for The Lord to help me show kindness and love in everything I do. Sometimes it's hard because the world can be cruel, but we need to be kind anyway. Love people anyway. I created love and peace cookies because they made me think of the 1970s, when people were struggling so badly to come together and there were lots of Summer Love & Peace movements. We can come together today, and cookies are a start. Spread kindness like sprinkles.

From the kitchen	From the drawer
Bunny head- (turned into peace fingers) and circle-shaped cookies Batch of buttercream	Tips 125, 12, 18, 349, 5, and 2 Piping bags Couplers Offset angled spatula Brown, dusty rose, green, turquoise, yellow orange, and white food coloring

Peace Hand Instructions

1. Use tip 5 and any skin color shade, and outline the cookie and fill it in. Pipe with a steady stream of pressure back and forth all the way down. Hold the bag at a 45° angle so the buttercream flows out like a tube of toothpaste.
2. Use an angled spatula and smooth the surface of the buttercream.
3. Pipe two fingers of the left of the hand so they are curved over to meet in the middle of the palm. Fill in the fingers like you filled in the hand and then smooth the fingers, but don't push the buttercream into the palm—you want the fingers to stand out.
4. Pipe a thumb and fill it in. Make the tip of the thumb close the peace sign with the other two fingers. Use the spatula to smooth the thumb.

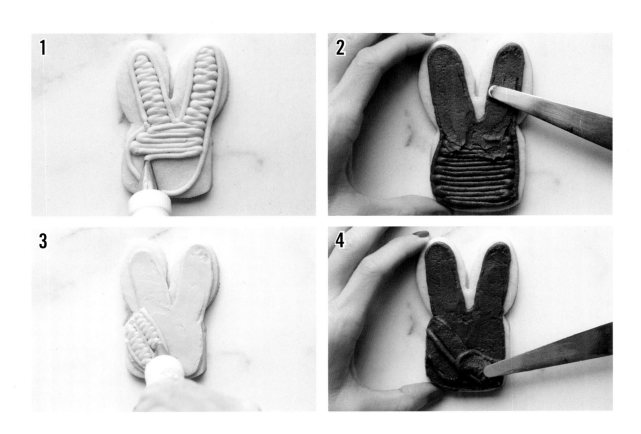

Continued on next page

Peace Flower Symbol Instructions

1. Use a light dusty rose buttercream and tip 18 to pipe little rosettes. Start piping and pull the buttercream down, then around in a circle, and then stop when you get back down at the bottom. Make 5 rosettes, spread out on the cookie, to start the peace sign.

2. Switch to a deeper dusty rose buttercream, also with tip 18 attached, and sporadically pipe rosettes around in the peace sign design.

3. Keep tip 18, but use light turquoise and make little bursts of buttercream so they look like stars. Pipe ¼ inch off the cookie and hold the piping bag straight up and down, squeeze buttercream, and stop, pulling up to cut off the buttercream.

4. Using yellow and tip 2, pipe a dollop of buttercream and pipe small dots on top of the mound to create a raised flower. Do this sporadically while keeping the peace sign shape.

5. Use tip 5 and white buttercream to make five small bursts of buttercream and put a yellow dot in the center using tip 2 to make tiny daisies. Once all the flowers are added, it will look like a peace sign.

6. Use green buttercream and tip 349 to make small leaves around the cookie. Pipe with the beak facing down. Squeeze small bursts of buttercream and then stop before you pull away.

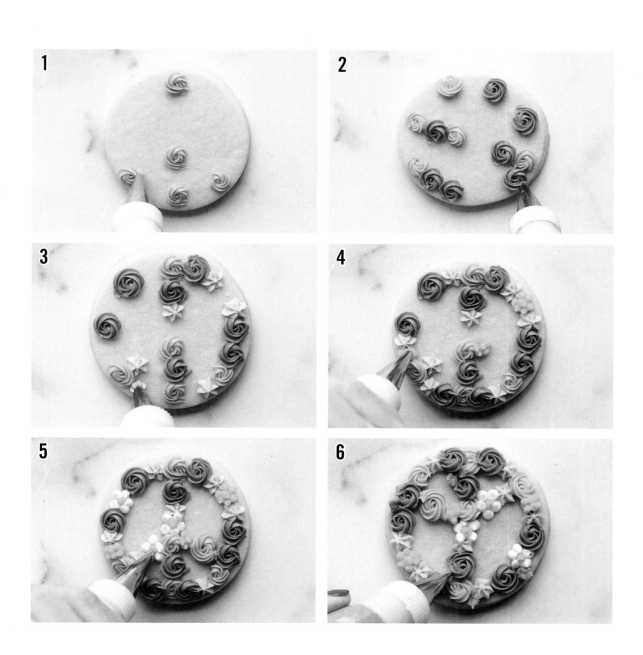

Continued on next page

Peace Symbol with Flowers Instructions

1. Use tip 12 and light turquoise to pipe a peace sign. Pipe holding the piping bag ¼ inch off the cookie and tilt the bag slightly toward you so the bag is angled. Squeeze with a steady stream of pressure to pipe the peace sign by rounding the cookie and piping a line straight through the center. Pipe up from the bottom right and go off center to the middle line of the cookie. Do the same thing to the other side to make the perfect peace sign.

2. With the dusty rose buttercream and tip 18, pipe small rosettes at the top right and the bottom left of the peace sign. Pipe holding the bag slightly angled and pipe down, around, and back to the top for each rosette.

3. With yellow buttercream and tip 2, pipe small clusters of buttercream to make little raised flowers.

4. Add in a couple dark dusty rose rosettes with tip 18.

5. With white and tip 5, pipe 5 small bursts of buttercream and leave the center open. Do this in the center of the peace sign. Pipe yellow with tip 2 for the center of the daisy.

6. With tip 349 and green buttercream, pipe small leaves to fill in between the flowers to add a little greenery.

MASTER TIP

Change the colors to be more vibrant if you'd like. Dip spatula in hot water and quickly dry before smoothing the peace fingers to make a really smooth surface.

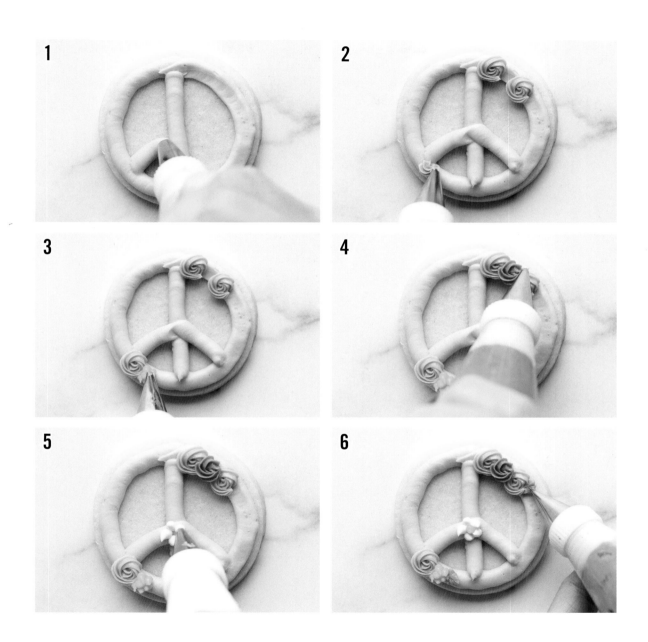

Continued on next page

Daisy Instructions

1. Use tip 125 and white buttercream. Start at the edge of the cookie with the wide end at the edge facing away from you. Hold the tip about ¼ inch off the cookie and squeeze until the buttercream billows out the sides to form the petal. Slowly pull in toward the center and slowly stop squeezing. Continue around the cookie until it's full.
2. Use tip 2 and yellow buttercream. Make a circle in the center and fill it in. Pipe small bursts of buttercream all around the top to make the center look realistic.

Daisy Side View Instructions

1. Use tip 125 and white buttercream. Start at the edge of the cookie with the wide end at the edge facing away from you. Hold the tip about ¼ inch off the cookie and squeeze until the buttercream billows out the sides to form the petal. Slowly pull in toward the center and slowly stop squeezing. Do this to make petals on half of the cookie.
2. Use tip 2 and yellow buttercream. Make a half circle in the center and fill it in. Pipe small bursts of buttercream all around the top to make the top of the yellow floral discs.

Psalm 34:18 The LORD is close to the brokenhearted and saves those who are crushed in spirit.

Fall

Bookworm

page 230

Harvest Pumpkins

page 236

Bookworm

These cookies remind me of Reese, and I'll tell you why, but first I have to tell you a story about me. When I was little, I envied people with glasses; I wanted them so badly, but my vision was 20/20. I decided in order to get the pink-framed glasses I wanted, I must fake the eye exam. It worked, and I got the cutest pink-framed glasses and wore them for a solid six months before my eyesight magically corrected itself.

So back to Reese—when she was little, she told me that it was a little hard for her to see things, which I, the eyesight fibber, had a hard time believing. Even after she failed the eye exam and the doctor prescribed glasses, I still didn't fully believe she needed glasses because of my own fib. The day we picked up her cute blue-framed glasses, she looked out the window of the car and, in the sweetest voice, said, "Mama, I can read those signs now. This is so cool." Needless to say, I felt terrible that I hadn't believed her. Reese was always my reader who loved books so much. That's why these bookworm cookies remind me of my sweet girl with glasses.

Summer comes to an end and fall is quickly approaching. These back-to-school book-worm cookies are so darling and make the perfect sweet treat to get the school year off to a great start. Giving these to teachers would be really smart!

From the kitchen	From the drawer
Present-, oval-, rectangle-, and circle-shaped cookies Batch of buttercream	Tips 47, 12, 352, 5, and 2 Piping bags Couplers Offset angled spatula Red, green, yellow, black, and white food coloring

Bookworm Face Instructions

1. Using green buttercream and tip 12, pipe around the cookie's edge in a circle and fill in the cookie. Use an offset spatula to smooth the buttercream.

2. With black and tip 2, pipe two circles for the frames of the glasses and make a line to connect the bridge and the temples.

3. Use white buttercream with tip 12 and pipe dollops of white for the worm's eyes.

4. Using tip 2 with black, pipe two dots for the eyes and a small, happy grin for the worm's face.

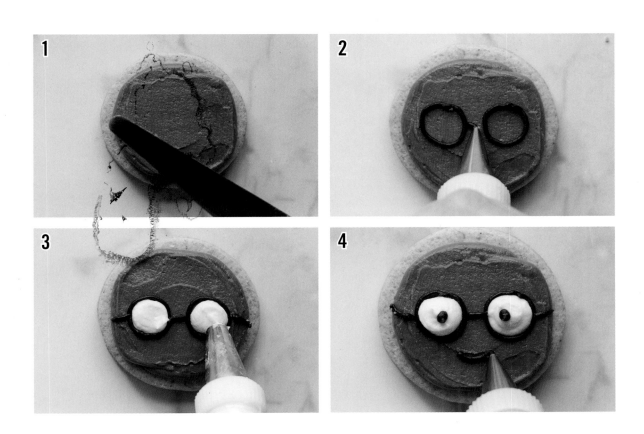

Continued on next page

Bookworm Instructions

1. Using green and tip 12, start at one end of the oval-shaped cookie and hold the piping bag ¼ inch off the cookie. Pipe in bursts of buttercream and round the top so the point doesn't form like on a Hershey's kiss. Pipe four dollops and then a larger one for the head, and round that off, as well.

2. Use tip 2 and black buttercream. Pipe two circles for the eyes and a bridge for the frames. Pipe a smile under the glasses.

3. Fill in the circles with white buttercream and tip 5, then use black to make tiny dots in the center of the white eyeballs.

Book Instructions

1. Pipe green or red buttercream with tip 47, making a rectangular shape. Use an offset spatula to smooth the surface.

2. Use white and tip 5 to pipe a line for the book's spine.

3. Use tip 2 and black buttercream to write MATH on the cover of the book.

Apple Instructions

1. Use tip 5 and white buttercream to pipe an outline of an apple and fill it in. Take an offset spatula and smooth out the apple.

2. With brown buttercream and tip 5, pipe the seeds. Pipe a small amount of buttercream off center and then point the edge out. Repeat on the opposite side to make two seeds in the center of the apple.

3. Take red buttercream and pipe a border around the outside of the white to look like the apple's skin.

4. With tip 5 and green, pipe one straight stem coming from the top of the apple. Then, attach tip 352 and pipe a leaf. Hold the beak facing down, start squeezing, and as the buttercream billows out, move slightly back, stop squeezing, and pull away.

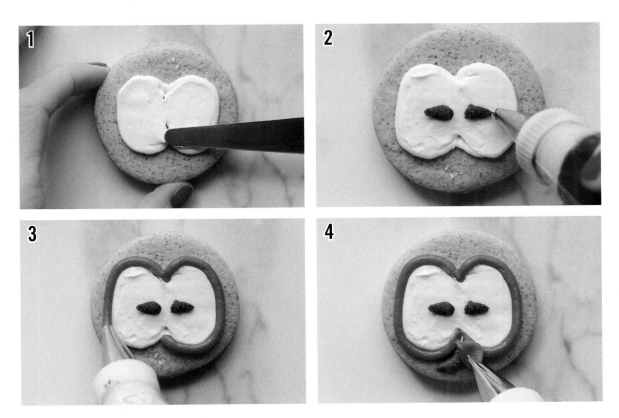

Continued on next page

Stack of Books with Worm Instructions

1. Use tip 47 and yellow buttercream. Pipe with the smooth end upward and the ridged end facing the cookie base. Pipe two lines of buttercream from one end of the book to the other. Take an offset spatula and smooth the two thick lines together flat. Pipe two lines of red just under the yellow, also using tip 47.

2. Smooth the red, as well.

3. Using tip 47 and green buttercream, pipe one final strip at the bottom of the cookie.

4. With tip 5 and green buttercream, hold the piping bag ¼ inch off the cookie base. Pipe, with a burst of buttercream, small dots on the top of the book stack for the worm's body. Pipe one large one for the head.

5. Use black and tip 2, and pipe two circles for the eyes, keeping some room in the center for white buttercream. With tip 5 and white buttercream, pipe buttercream to fill the center of the black frames to make eyes. Use tip 2 and black again and make small dots for the center of the eye.

6. Take tip 2 and pipe vertical lines for each spine of the books, two lines per book.

MASTER TIP

Make the books any color. Add little hair sprouts coming from the top of the worm's head to give it character. Write any subject on the book covers.

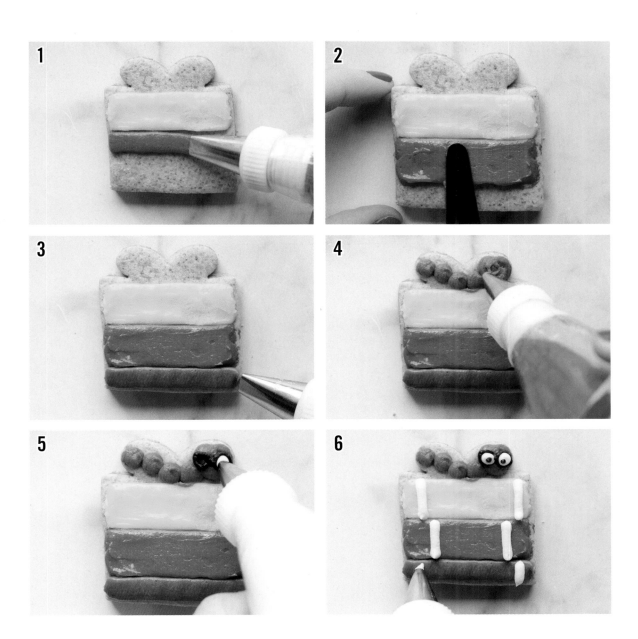

Harvest Pumpkins

I made pumpkin tops with textured tips for a fun twist on one of my famous cookie designs. The beautiful deep purple is a treat to look at. I also like that the view is shifted to the side a little and not a completely aerial view. I always love seeing things from a different point of view.

From the kitchen
Circle-shaped cookies
Batch of buttercream

From the drawer
Tips 199, 32, 12, and 18
Piping bags
Couplers
Offset angled spatula
Orange, green, purple, pink, and brown
    food coloring

Purple-Textured Pumpkin Instructions

1. Start piping with tip 199 and purple buttercream. Start at the top center. Hold the piping bag tilted toward you at a 45° angle. Have the tip almost touching the cookie and squeeze a large amount of buttercream, let it billow out and upward, pull in toward the middle of the cookie, and go a little farther but not to the very bottom. Pipe more streams of buttercream on either side and work your way down the cookie. You're creating a side view of the pumpkin.

2. Pipe around, making the pumpkin wide. Each section of the pumpkin will get shorter as you work your way to the edges of the cookie. The top of the cookie where the buttercream comes together will be slightly overlapping the sides to create dimension.

3. Use tip 18 with brown buttercream to pipe the stem. Squeeze and pull up while squeezing and then stop. Pull the bag up for a little pumpkin stem.

Light-Green Textured Pumpkin Instructions

1. Start piping with tip 32 and green buttercream. Start at the top center. Hold the piping bag tilted toward you at a 45° angle. Have the tip almost touching the cookie and squeeze a large amount of buttercream, let it billow out and upward, pull in toward the middle of the cookie, and go a little farther but not to the very bottom. Pipe more streams of buttercream on either side and work your way down the cookie. You're creating a side view of the pumpkin.

2. As you work your way to the sides, make it look rounded, as pictured.

3. Then pipe small bursts and bring it to where the stem will be. It will be the center of your pumpkin but not the center of the cookie because it's offset a little to create the side view.

4. Turn the cookie around and use tip 18 with brown buttercream to pipe the stem. Squeeze and pull up while squeezing and then stop. Pull the bag away to reveal a sweet little pumpkin stem.

MASTER TIP

For the pink and orange pumpkins, use tip 12 and the same technique you used for the textured pumpkins. Practice piping on a plate before starting your cookies. This is similar to the shell or teardrop technique, but it's piping longer shells when starting and getting smaller on the sides and top of pumpkin. Make these any colors. Light blues would be gorgeous to add.

Spooky Halloween
page 240

Pies
page 248

Spooky Halloween

My Grandma Loopie and Pop Pop always put together Oso's scariest Halloween house. Here's the story: Each year, my grandparents would tell us that they were going on a vacation right before Halloween and that very strange people would be house sitting. They always said, "Don't be scared to come down, make sure to get candy. I think they will have king-sized bars." Picture a long gravel driveway in the pitch dark, in the middle of Oso, secluded and really spooky.

My mom piled me and my three sisters in the car. We were little and scared. One of us, or maybe all of us, cried as we slowly drove down the driveway, anticipating who was going to be housesitting that year.

Grandma Loopie was terrifying—she always dressed up really creepy, white-faced and bloody-mouthed to look like the undead. Pop Pop always wore the same scary mask that covered half his face with fangs that came down, very devilish. Each year, they planned a new stunt to terrify the kids of Oso and, most importantly, their grandkids.

One year, Grandma Loopie hid her own head under a silver dome that we lifted up to find her, gruesome and hissing. Uncle Steve joined in the scare each year with some weapon, too, whether he was running out of the bushes with a chainsaw to chase kids or running around with a machete, screaming. Each year, we came back for more—the whole town of Oso came down just to get scared. I think that's where my sisters and I inherited our amusement with creepiness and scaring kids on Halloween.

From the kitchen

Ghost-, bone-, and circle-shaped
  cookies
Batch of flooding buttercream
1/2 batch of buttercream

From the drawer

Tips 4 and 1A
Piping bags
Couplers
Tipless piping bags
Black, white, and red food coloring
Candy eyes
White nonpareils
Toothpick or scribe tool
Food-safe paint brush
Latex gloves

Mummy Instructions

1. Use tip 47 and regular buttercream. Pipe with the smooth edge upward. Pipe all the way around the outside of the cookie for the border. For the top half, pipe some crisscross strips going from one end to the other. The top half will be smaller because it's only covering the forehead of the mummy. Leave space for the eyes.

2. Pipe the same crisscross strips from one end to the other to fill the bottom of the mummy, from the nose down.

3. On the right top side, pipe strips from the tip that drape down the side for loose bandages.

4. Pipe two small dots of buttercream for each eye and put on the candy eyes for the mummy.

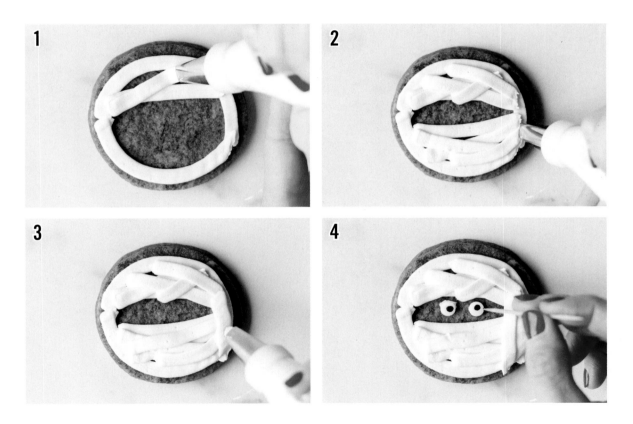

Continued on next page

Count Dracula Instructions

1. Using a circle cookie and flooding buttercream in white, outline and pipe a widow's peak hairline for the Count Dracula. Use a squeeze bottle or a tipless piping bag. If using a squeeze bottle, use a very small tip. I used a 2 here.
2. Take a toothpick and swirl out any bumps or air bubbles.
3. Take black flooding buttercream and flood in the widow's peak.
4. Use the toothpick again and make the peak pointy and the edges crisp.
5. Let cookie dry for 15 minutes and then pipe a mouth and fill it in with black flooding buttercream.
6. Use the toothpick to make the mouth points sharp and defined. Pull the black buttercream with the toothpick to make it come to a point in the corners.
7. Use white flooding buttercream and tipless bag and make two tiny dots for the eyes and attach the candy eyeballs. Pipe two teeth right on top of the black mouth.
8. Use the toothpick to get the tips of the teeth sharp by dipping it in the white and pulling it downward. Don't push into the black; just skim the surface.

MASTER TIP

Make the cookie set fun by adding glitter and sprinkles. Omit the red blood spatter if it's too creepy for you. The mummy and the ghost can be pink for a more feminine touch. Use a large piece of parchment paper or plastic wrap under the bone cookie to prevent a massive mess with the red splatter.

Continued on next page

Spider's Web Instructions

1. Outline and fill the round cookie with white flooding buttercream.
2. Take a toothpick and swirl around the edges to get a clean-looking circle.
3. Take a tiny bit of black flooding buttercream and mix it with white flooding buttercream to get a gray. Use the gray buttercream in a tipless piping bag or squeeze bottle and pipe a thin swirl from the center, leading out. Make it thin and tight.
4. Take the toothpick and put the tip in the center. Pull the gray from the center straight to the outside to make a webbed look. Continue to do this all the way around the cookie, not too close to each other.
5. Sprinkle white nonpareils on the web. Use black flooding buttercream and make a little spider in the corner of the web.
6. Use the toothpick to make the legs of the spider pointy. Pull the black slightly outward to get the shape.

Continued on next page

Ghost Instructions

1. Take the gray flooding buttercream and use the paintbrush to paint on the cookie where the face would be.

2. Use white flooding buttercream and make circles for the eyes and one for the mouth. Outline the ghost.

3. Fill in the ghost from top to bottom. Use a steady stream of pressure back and forth all the way down the cookie to fill the ghost.

4. Use a toothpick or scribe to swirl away any bumps and to make the edges of the ghost sharp and crisp.

Bone Instructions

1. Use tip 1A and white buttercream. Hold the piping bag about ¼ inch off the cookie. Pipe with the bag straight up and down to get a flatter flow of buttercream. Pipe the first end in a V shape, then down the center, and then pipe the second end in an arrow shape.

2. Put on latex gloves. Take red food coloring, put a drop in a small bowl. Add in two drops of water. Dip paintbrush in, mix, and then splatter it on the cookie. Take your thumb and pull back the bristles and let go to fling the red. Add as much or as little as you want of the red.

Fang Bite Instructions

1. Using white flooding buttercream, outline a round cookie and fill it in. Squeeze a steady stream of pressure back and forth all the way down the center. Let set for 20 minutes.

2. Use a toothpick to make two holes in the center of the white slightly crusted flooding buttercream. This is the fang bite.

3. Take red food coloring and add a drop to a small bowl. Add in a couple drops of water. Use the paintbrush and mix it up. Paint red around the hole and make it drip down a little so it looks like dripping blood from a vampire bite. Gently shaking it down the cookie works great, too.

Pies

Pies are a staple for the holidays, especially Thanksgiving. If I'm being honest, my husband and I would have pie every night. My Grandma Loopie was famous for her pies, and I loved them, too. Pie was one of the first things I made on my own as a young baker, and I've rocked every pie since. Cookies that look like pies? Yes, please!

From the kitchen	**From the drawer**
Whole pie-shaped cookies	Tips 2, 4, 12 18, and 47
Batch of flooding buttercream	Piping bags
1/2 batch of buttercream	Couplers
	Tipless piping bags
	Brown, orange, gray (or a dash of black), white, and red food coloring
	Toothpick or scribe tool
	Offset spatula
	Ground cinnamon
	Sugar crystals

Pie Tin Instructions

1. Use gray flooding buttercream by mixing a tiny bit of black into white until desired shade is achieved. Use a tipless piping bag or a squeeze bottle with a tiny tip 2 attached. Pipe around the bottom of the pie where the tin would be. Use steady pressure to fill it in.

2. Use a scribe tool or toothpick to swirl around the edges to make them straight and get out any bumps or bubbles. Do this quickly so buttercream doesn't start to crust.

Apple Pie Instructions

1. Follow steps 1 and 2 from the Pie Tin instructions and allow to dry for 30 minutes. Add a small amount of brown to white to make a light tan buttercream, and set aside. Then, mix regular buttercream with some cinnamon to make it look like apple pie filling. We need both for this cookie. Fill piping bag with the cinnamon in it and attach tip 4. Pipe buttercream in the top part of the cookie for the apple pie filling. Use an offset spatula to smooth it a little.

2. Using the tan buttercream and also tip 4, pipe four teardrop shapes for the slits in the crust. Then outline the top of the crust for the pie.

3. Fill in the crust back and forth until it's filled but leave the slits open.

4. Use tip 12 and the tan buttercream and pipe on the crust that borders the pie just slightly over the tin. Make small wave motions to give it a crimped effect.

5. Sprinkle crust with sugar crystals.

Continued on next page

Cherry Pie Instructions

1. Follow steps 1 and 2 from the Pie Tin instructions and allow to dry for 30 minutes. Use red buttercream with tip 12. Hold piping bag straight up and down and about ¼ inch off the base of the cookie. Pipe until the buttercream billows out and then stop squeezing, twist bag to allow the buttercream to swirl off and flatten, and then pull away. If you stop squeezing and pull straight up, it will have a Hershey's kiss pointed top effect.

2. Take very light brown or tan colored buttercream and use tip 47. Position the smooth side up. and pipe diagonally from the top of the cherry pie to the tin. Give a little space between each strip of crust for the lattice weave.

3. Pipe diagonally in the opposite direction to complete the lattice weave.

4. Turn cookie upside down, attach tip 18 to white buttercream, and pipe a small whipped cream swirl at the top of the pie.

Pumpkin Pie Instructions

1. Follow steps 1 and 2 from the Pie Tin instructions, and allow to dry for 30 minutes. Use one part brown and two parts orange to make pumpkin pie orange in buttercream. Use the orange buttercream and tip 12 in a piping bag. Hold piping tip ¼ inch off cookie, and in the middle, pipe one solid line for pumpkin.

2. Use an offset spatula to smooth the buttercream.

3. Take tan or very light brown buttercream with tip 12. Pipe under the pumpkin pie color to make the crust. Make a slight wave as you're piping to look like pie crust.

4. Use white buttercream and tip 18. Turn the cookie upside down and pipe three swirls for the whipped cream.

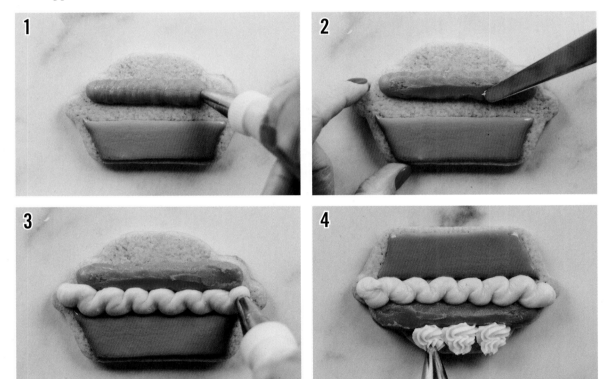

MASTER TIP

Use the flooding buttercream to pipe the pie tins first, one after the other. It will make it so much easier. Change the pumpkin color to dark brown for chocolate cream pie or yellow for lemon.

Pie Slices

page 254

Turkey Dinner

page 258

Pie Slices

We have good friends who own the best pie shop in the Pacific Northwest—Mike's their biggest fan. Inspired by them, I've decided to turn my sugar cookies into decorated pie slices. Everyone that knows Mike is aware he can't stop at one slice. I had a few Pi-deas and made three different pie slices.

From the kitchen	**From the drawer**
Pie slice–shaped cookies	Tips 4, 12, 18, and 47
Batch of buttercream	Piping bags
	Couplers
	Brown, orange, white, and red food coloring
	Offset spatula
	Ground cinnamon
	Sugar crystals

Apple Pie Slice Instructions

1. Add a small amount of brown to white buttercream to make a light tan buttercream, and set aside. Then, mix regular buttercream with some cinnamon to make it look like apple pie filling. We need both for this cookie. Use tip 4 with the cinnamon buttercream and pipe the cookie, but leave the crust and the edges of the cookie unfrosted at this time. Use an offset spatula to smooth the buttercream for the pie filling.

2. With tan buttercream and tip 12, pipe the bottom crust and left side crust.

3. Use tip 4 and pipe two slits in the top crust and outline the crust where the top of the pie would be.

4. Outline back and forth to fill in the top crust, careful not to fill in the open slits. Let the pie filling peek through.

5. Use tip 12 again to pipe the top crust in a wavy motion to look like crimping in the crust.

6. Sprinkle sugar crystals on the crust.

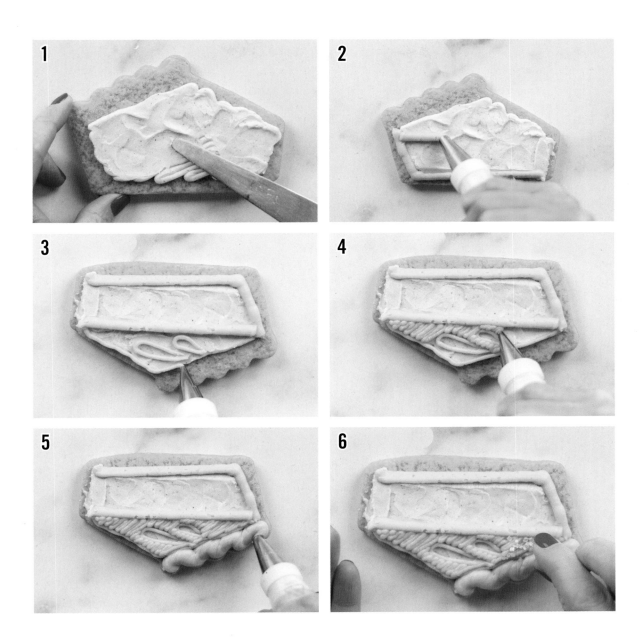

Continued on next page

Cherry Pie Slice Instructions

1. Take tan buttercream with tip 12 and pipe the middle crust, the bottom, and the left side. Leave the far right open.

2. Use tip 12 with red buttercream and make dollops of frosting to fill the center. Also pipe these dollops and overlap a little at the top.

3. Use tan buttercream and tip 47. Position the flat, smooth side of the tip facing upward and the ridged side toward the red buttercream. Pipe lines diagonally on the top part of the red cherries. Leave a little space between each strip. To make a lattice weave, now pipe the tan buttercream in the opposite direction on the top, as pictured.

4. Use tip 12 again with tan buttercream and pipe the crust edge, using a slight wave motion to look like the crimping of the crust.

Pumpkin Pie Slice Instructions

1. Using tan buttercream and tip 12, pipe the bottom, middle, and left side of the crust.

2. Make pumpkin pie buttercream by using one part brown and two parts orange. Also with tip 12, but using pumpkin pie orange-colored buttercream, fill the center and use an offset spatula to smooth the buttercream. Turn cookie bottom-side up, and pipe the part of the pie that is unfrosted at the top. Leave the top crust unfrosted. Use the offset spatula to smooth the buttercream.

3. Using tip 12 and tan buttercream, pipe along the crust and make a slight wave motion to look like crimping.

4. Use tip 18 and white buttercream to make a whipped cream–looking swirl on the top.

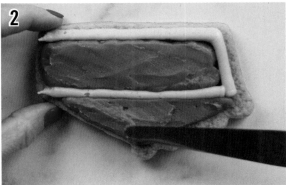

MASTER TIP

Make the cherry pie blue for blueberry. Make the pumpkin pie deep brown for chocolate cream, or yellow for lemon. So many fun Pi-deas to create delicious pie cookies.

Turkey Dinner

My memories of my childhood Thanksgivings, up until carrying on traditions with my own family, are all so special. I remember my grandma would talk to her turkey as she was rubbing the cold, seasoned skin with generous amounts of butter, prepping the fowl for roasting. It was always so funny to me; I didn't understand why she was talking to a dead bird. As an adult, I realized she was just putting positive energy out to make sure the turkey cooks through. I like to turn up music, dance in the kitchen, and cook with my mom, sisters, and daughter. You can't go wrong with matching turkey dinner cookies complete with the whole turkey, a leg, mashed potatoes, and brown gravy with a side of peas and carrots.

From the kitchen

Whole turkey-, turkey leg-, and-round shaped cookies
Flooding buttercream
$\frac{1}{2}$ batch of buttercream

From the drawer

Tips 5, 12, 104 and 47
Piping bags
Couplers
Tipless piping bags or squeeze bottle
Toothpick or scribe tool
Brown, orange, green, and white food coloring
Offset spatula
Gold sugar crystals

Whole Turkey Instructions

1. Take tip 5 and regular white buttercream and pipe two lines at the bottom of the turkey cookie to make a platter.

2. Using brown flooding buttercream in a tipless piping bag or a squeeze bottle with the smallest hole, outline the turkey and fill it in with a steady stream until the turkey is filled up. Use a toothpick or scribe tool to swirl out any lumps.

3. Sprinkle on gold sugar crystals.

4. Use tip 5 and white buttercream again and make a bone at the end of the turkey leg by squeezing a large amount of pressure until the buttercream billows out and then pull downward toward the turkey.

5. Use brown flooding buttercream again and finish the turkey by adding to the leg.

6. Use green buttercream and pipe lettuce under the turkey, right at the platter. Have the wide end of the tip toward the cookie and the skinny end facing up and out to make the ruffle of the lettuce thin. Pipe all the way down.

Continued on next page

Peas and Carrots Instructions

1. Use tip 12 and green buttercream. To pipe the peas, squeeze a large amount the buttercream in pea-sized or larger dots, overlap, and fill up the cookie.

2. Use tip 47 and orange buttercream with the smooth edge facing upward. Pipe little square carrot chunks sporadically around the mound of peas.

 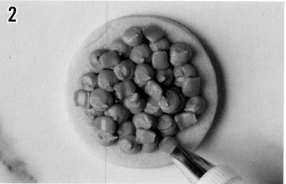

Turkey Leg Instructions

1. Use white buttercream with tip 12 attached. Start by holding the tip ¼ inch off the cookie. Squeeze in the corner of the bone and then pull back and stop squeezing. Repeat on the opposite side.

2. Take the brown flooding buttercream and pipe the outline for the turkey leg and then quickly fill it in. Use a toothpick or scribe tool to swirl out any lumps.

3. Add gold sugar crystals to the brown part of the cookie.

Mashed Potatoes and Brown Gravy Instructions

1. Using white buttercream and tip 12, pipe mashed potatoes by squeezing and making a wavy motion around the cookie.

2. Take the offset spatula and smooth but make it look like mashed potatoes. Keep it sloppy.

3. Use brown flooding buttercream and pipe gravy that spills over the mashed potatoes.

MASTER TIP

Make the gravy lighter for turkey gravy. Add a dollop of yellow buttercream to the mashed potatoes for butter.

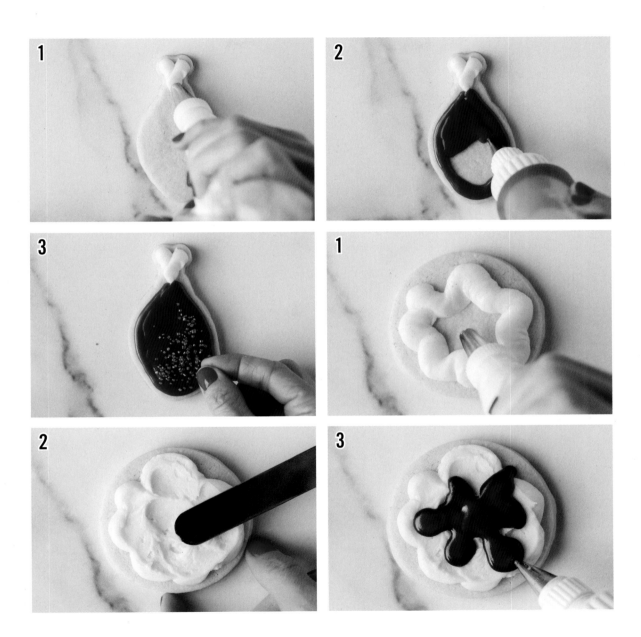

Turkey

page 263

Turkey

I love decorating turkeys for Thanksgiving; these are so darling, and they have a lot of personality. I should tell these turkeys not to look next door because the other turkey cookies are a full COOKED dinner.

From the kitchen	**From the drawer**
Turkey-shaped cookies	Tips 104, 8B, 2A, 12, 18, 2, 5, and 349
Batch of buttercream	Piping bags
	Couplers
	Brown, orange, yellow, white, green, and red food coloring
	Sugar crystals

Turkey Instructions

1. Use red buttercream with tip 104 attached. Start piping in at the top layer of feathers. Position the wide end of the tip facing the edge of the cookie and the skinny end toward you. Start squeezing until the buttercream billows out the sides and slowly pull down and stop squeezing to make each feather.

2. Just under the first layer of red feathers, take orange buttercream with tip 104 and pipe the same technique all the way along the second layer.

Continued on next page

3. Complete the feathers by adding yellow with tip 104, and pipe feathers for the third and smallest layer.

4. Take tip 8B and dark brown buttercream to make the body. Start piping in the middle of the yellow feathers. Hold piping bag straight up and down about ¼ inch off the yellow feathers. Squeeze a large amount of buttercream, slowly pull the piping bag toward the bottom of the cookie where the body will stop, and give it one more big squeeze for the body. Be careful because it can look a little poopy if you're not!

5. Use tip 5 and white buttercream and pipe two dots for the eyes.

6. Take tip 2 and black buttercream to pipe smaller dots on top of the white.

7. Use orange buttercream with tip 349 to make a small beak on the turkey. Squeeze and release just under the eyes.

8. Use tip 5 and red buttercream to pipe a small wattle on the side of the beak and make it hang down ever so slightly.

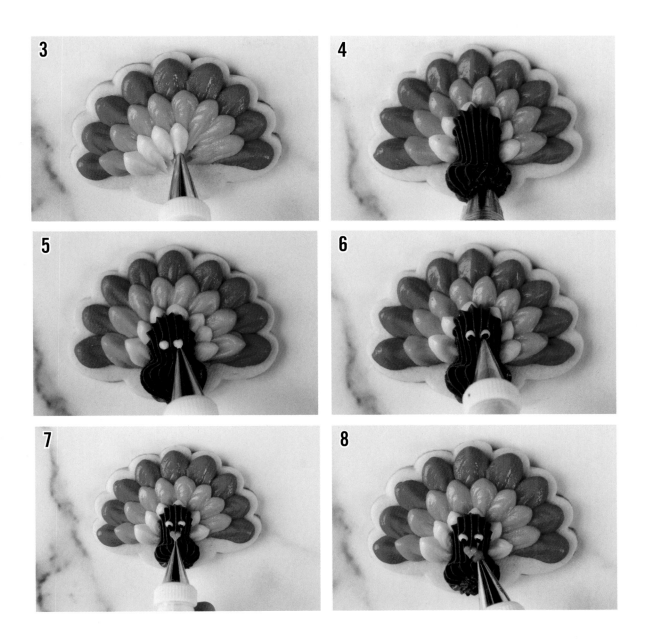

Continued on next page

Leaf Instructions

1. Use tip 104 with light green buttercream. Start at the bottom and work your way up. To pipe, hold the skinny end facing the edge of the cookie, away from you. Have the wide end facing toward you. Start squeezing and make small, rounding motions as you make each leaf part.
2. Turn the cookie to the side and repeat this technique down the opposite side to complete the leaf.

MASTER TIP

To mix light green, I mix my darker green first and then use the remnants of the green in the bowl to color the next cup of buttercream I add, which will make light green. Make the turkey feathers tan, white, and yellow for a more neutral look.

Cranberries Instructions

1. Make the leaves on the berries by using green buttercream and tip 104. Start by having the wide end facing upward toward the edge of the cookie. Start squeezing until the buttercream billows out and slowly pull down and stop. Continue to make three leaves.

2. Use tip 2A and red buttercream, hold piping bag ½ inch off the cookie, and squeeze a large amount of buttercream for the first berry. Round the top by making a sweeping motion with the piping bag so the end of the tip skims the top off and is flat, otherwise you'll have a Hershey's kiss effect. Pipe two more berries the same way.

3. Use tip 18 and white buttercream to make small bursts on the center of each cranberry.

4. Sprinkle with sugar crystals for sugared cranberries.

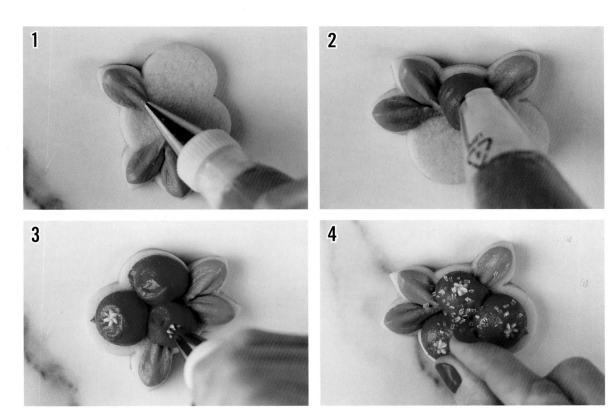

"If you see someone without a smile today, give 'em yours."
—Dolly Parton

Cosmos

page 272

Poppies & Dahlias

page 274

Cosmos

Cosmos are one of my favorite flowers; they're delicate and vibrant. I love how even the white ones can liven up any bouquet. I remember my mom would plant these in her garden in Oso. Cosmos can survive in poor soil conditions but have slender stems, so they are strong and also dainty. Bees and butterflies love them. I think I love them even more in buttercream.

From the kitchen
Round-shaped cookies
Batch of buttercream

From the drawer
Tips 104 and 2
Piping bags
Couplers
Pink, purple, yellow, and white gel food coloring.

Cosmo Flower Instructions

1. Use tip 104 and pink buttercream. Turn the piping tip so the wide end is facing toward you and the skinny end is away from you. Start in the center of the cookie and slowly pull up. Stop when the skinny end reaches the outer edge of the cookie, squeeze, and make a straight petal by moving the piping bag straight over as you're squeezing. Make a slight motion with the piping bag in and out to make a ripple in the petal.

2. Slowly squeeze and then pull down toward the center, as pictured.

3. Repeat the technique to form more petals.

4. Continue to slowly squeeze, straight across petals and pulling down and inward.

5. Use tip 2 and bright yellow buttercream and make a round circle right in the center of the pink buttercream. Fill in the circle.

6. Make tiny dots all around the filled center to make the disk of the Cosmo.

MASTER TIP

Make these any beautiful bright color of your choice—make an array of Cosmos or add them into any flower set. They are simple and gorgeous. Make sure the skinny end is forming the end of the petals, otherwise they will be really thick. If they're too thick, simply flip the piping tip.

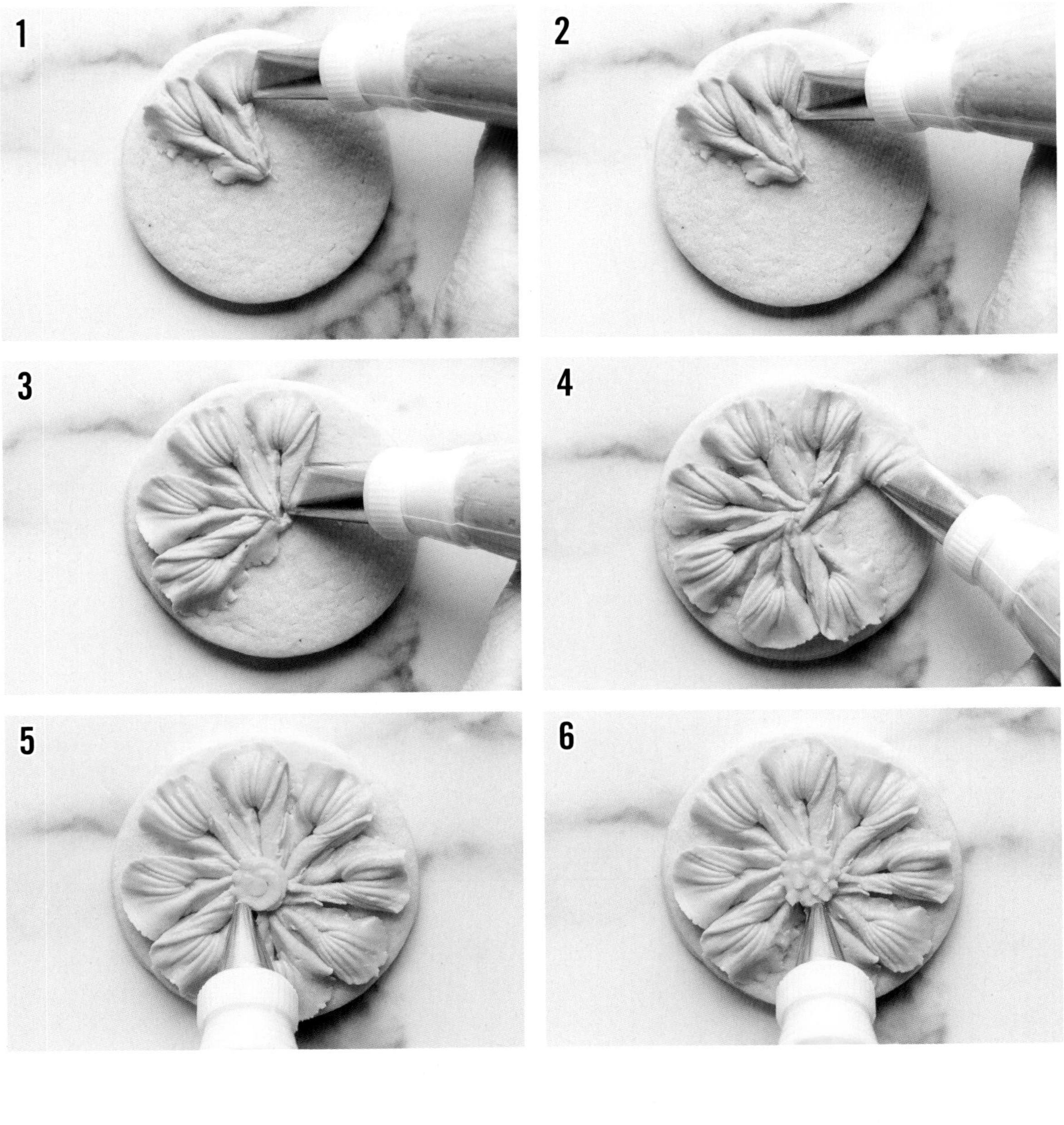
1
2
3
4
5
6

Poppies & Dahlias

This is a plate of bright beautifulness: Icelandic poppies, California Poppies, and Dahlias. Poppies are one of my favorite flowers, and I thought changing them up to include an orange Icelandic poppy would be a fresh idea. The California poppy takes my mind's eye to seeing fields of orange flowers spread through California.

I started growing Dahlias in my garden, and I've never been so proud. You guys, I've killed air plants, but I sure can grow a Dahlia. I love the pom Dahlias, too, and I added one to this set, so you're getting two different Dahlia flowers.

From the kitchen	From the drawer
Round-shaped cookies, 3–4 inches wide Batch of buttercream	Tips 104, 123, 125, 233, 143, 81, 12, 4, 21, 103, and 2 Piping bags Couplers Orange, green, and yellow gel food coloring.

Icelandic Poppy Instructions

1. Use tip 123 and light peach/orange buttercream. Achieve this color by adding a very small amount of orange to the white buttercream. Hold the piping tip with the wide end inward at the base of the cookie and the skinny end away from you to the outside of the cookie. Start piping the first petal, making small in-and-out motions to create the rippled, crepe-like texture in the petal.

2. Repeat this technique to create five petals on the base of the cookie. Make a slight rounding motion with a steady stream of pressure to make each rounded petal with the bunching motion to create the ripples.

3. Make a second layer of petals just slightly inwards and make each petal off-center so they are staggered and not right on top of each other. The second layer of petals will be smaller than the base layer.

4. With light green buttercream and tip 12, pipe a dollop of buttercream in the center of the poppy.

5. Next, use yellow buttercream and tip 21 to pipe a star right in the center of the green pistil. Gently squeeze and release.

6. Attach tip 4 and pipe all the way around the center to create stalk-like stamens. Start squeezing while pulling up to guide each part of the buttercream until you've made enough for the center of the poppy.

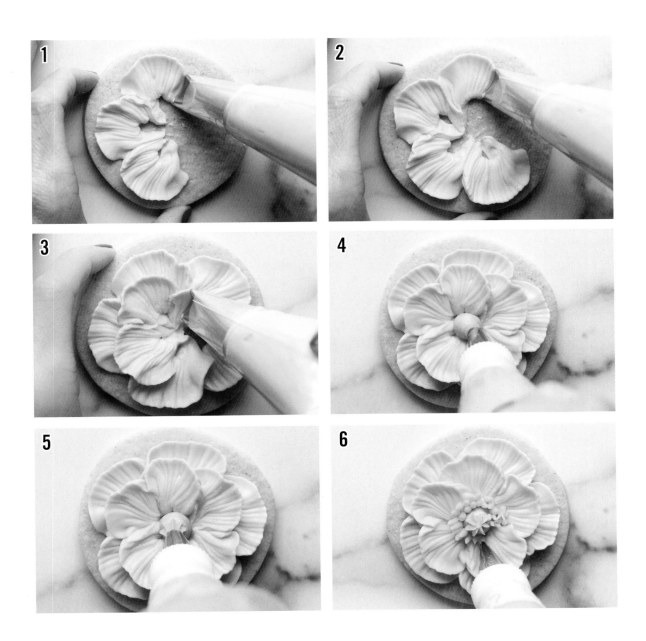

Continued on next page

California Poppy Top Instructions

1. Using bright orange and tip 125, hold the skinny end facing the edge of the cookie away from you and the wide end facing toward you. Squeeze one petal and then squeeze one on the opposite side to get perfectly placed petals. Pipe a third in the open spot to the left and the final one to the right. This petal is a simple, straight petal.

2. Use tip 233 and pipe a dollop of orange for grass-like buttercream in the center.

California Poppy Side Instructions

1. Use tip 104 and bright orange buttercream. Hold the skinny end away from you and the wide end toward you at the base of the cookie. Start squeezing at the top of the cookie and pipe a small petal. Carefully round your wrist to get a slight curve at the tip of the petal.

2. Move to either side of the first petal and pipe two more that meet in the middle and slightly overlap.

3. Use tip 2 and pipe stamen coming from the center of the poppy.

4. Using tip 4 and green buttercream, pipe a stem coming from the base of the petals to the edge of the cookie.

MASTER TIP

Change the colors of the buttercream to a pale pink and a bright pink. Change the poppies to red for Memorial Day. Use the poppy side view technique to make any rose or flower small bloom. Make the Dahlias multiple colors to offer a variety of flowers.

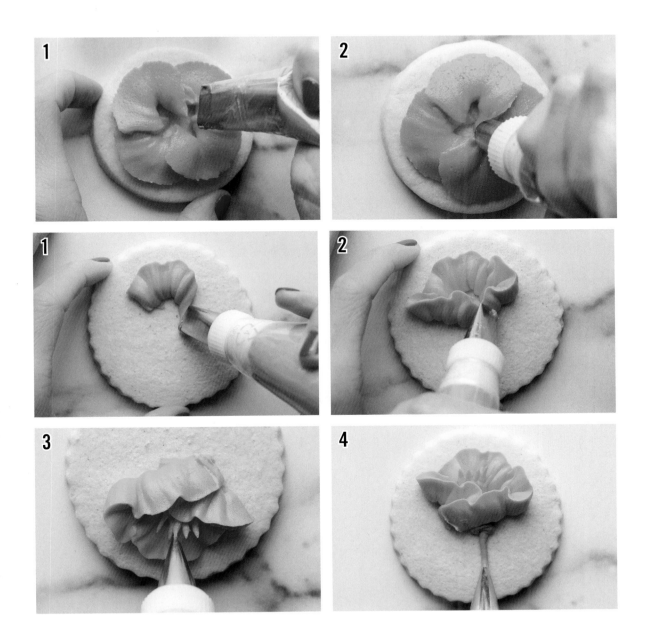

Continued on next page

Dahlia Instructions

1. Using tip 143 and orange buttercream, start piping on the outer part of the cookie but not the very edge. Hold the piping tip ¼ inch off the cookie, squeeze with a good amount of pressure while slowly pulling up, and then stop squeezing and pull away completely to break the buttercream.
2. Continue making layers of petals, working your way into the center, but leave a small space in the middle.
3. Switch to tip 81 and make small bursts of buttercream to fill in the very center.

Pom Dahlia Instructions

1. Use tip 103 and orange buttercream. Hold the skinny end of the tip facing away from you and the wide end toward you and at the base of the cookie. Have piping bag at a 45° angle. Start on the outer edge of the cookie, but don't pipe to the very edge. Start squeezing and pull up and down to make each small petal of the pom dahlia. Continue all the way around.
2. Do a second layer just slightly in from the first and go all the way around to meet back where you started. Continue to do this as you move into the center.
3. The center petals will be smaller and tighter. Keep piping until it's filled.

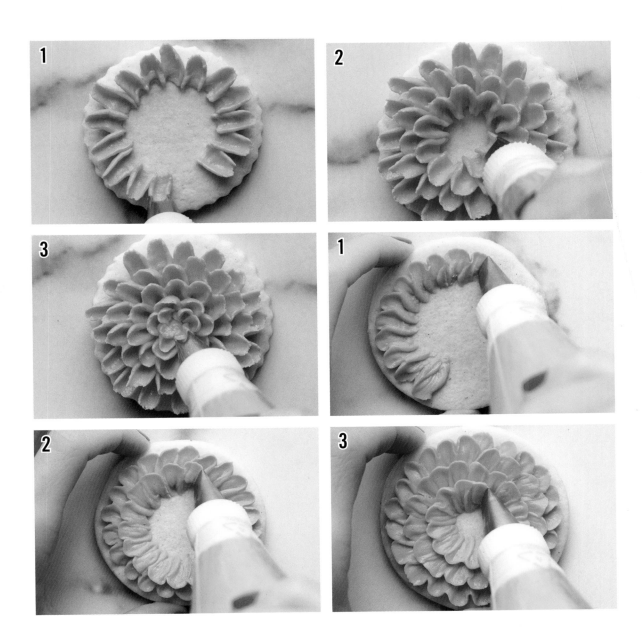

Dogwood
page 282

Zinnias
page 284

Dogwood

Dogwood flowers are often used as a symbol of rebirth and resurrection. Dogwoods are tall and large with similar strength to an oak tree, and the flowers that bloom are durable and can withstand various weather conditions. The Dogwood flowers are some of my favorites because of their simple beauty; they are easy to pipe in buttercream. Add a colored circle behind the flower by using the Freezer Frosting Method on page 31.

From the kitchen	**From the drawer**
Round-shaped cookies	Tips 104 and 2
Batch of buttercream	Piping bags
	Couplers
	White, green, and pink gel food coloring.

Dogwood Instructions

1. Use white buttercream and tip 104. Hold the skinny end of the tip facing the edge of the cookie away from you and the wide end toward you. Start piping and gently round your wrist to make each petal.
2. Pipe four petals total for the base of the flower.
3. With light pink and tip 2, pipe a small bit of color on the edge of each petal.
4. With two colors of green (light and a darker shade), attach tip 2 and pipe the stamen in the center with both greens. Make a cluster and pull upward with each one.

MASTER TIP

Make the petals a deeper pink for a variation of dogwood flower colors. Pipe the top and bottom petals and then the left and right for even petal placement.

Zinnias

The bright colors of the zinnia flower liven up any bouquet. They symbolize endurance and lasting friendship because they bloom until the fall frost. The center of each bloom is different, and I love that. Make an entire buttercream bouquet of Zinnias or add them to brighten up any cookie set.

From the kitchen	From the drawer
Round-shaped cookies, 3–4 inches wide Batch of buttercream	Tips 103, 2, and 18 Piping bags Couplers Purple, red, pink, and yellow gel food coloring.

Pink Zinnia Instructions

1. Use deep pink buttercream and tip 103. Hold the skinny end of the piping tip away from you and the wide end toward you at the base of the cookie. Hold the piping bag at a 45° angle and start piping at the edge of the cookie. Pipe small petals with a steady stream of pressure, slightly piping up and down while turning the cookie at the same time.

2. Make three layers of petals, one just slightly under the last, but keep the center open.

3. Attach tip 2 to the pink, pipe a dollop on the center, and then fill it with tiny dots to make the disk.

4. Using yellow buttercream with tip 18, pipe small bursts of buttercream to go around the disk.

Red Zinnia Instructions

1. Follow steps 1 and 2 from the Pink Zinnia instructions, but use red buttercream and tip 103. Pipe the middle layer of petals very small and tight to close the center.

2. Use tip 18 and yellow buttercream. Hold piping bag straight up and down, and squeeze little bursts of buttercream sporadically to make the center.

MASTER TIP

Make sure the skinny end is forming the tips of the petals or you will create a blob-like flower. Make bright yellow zinnias to add to any bouquet.

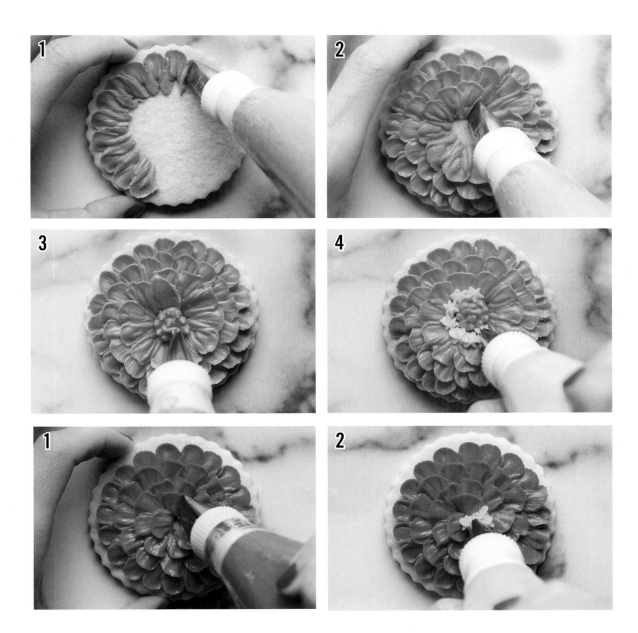

Lilacs & Hydrangeas

page 288

Camillas & Gardenias
page 292

Lilacs & Hydrangeas

These are easily one of my all-time favorite cookie sets. I love lilacs and hydrangeas. Every time the lilacs would bloom at my grandma's house, I could walk up the driveway and smell their sweet aroma on the wind. They have an early bloom, bursting from the branches they grow on. Hydrangeas are beautifully colorful flowers, as well, that grow full on their bush. The colors remind me of a garden party, so let's get gardening with buttercream.

From the kitchen	From the drawer
Round-shaped cookies, 3–4 inches wide Batch of buttercream	Tips 102, 21, and 366 Piping bags Couplers Purple, blue, pink, moss green, and green food coloring Blue and pink nonpareils

Lilac Instructions

1. With purple buttercream and tip 21, hold piping tip ¼ inch off the cookie straight up and down. Pipe bursts of buttercream in the shape of a lilac and then fill it in.

2. Attach tip 102. Hold piping bag straight up and down with the wide end pointed upward to the edge of the cookie. This will make a petal that is small and rounded. Hold close to the buttercream we piped for the base of the flowers. Pipe until the buttercream billows out of the sides and stop, pulling up to break the buttercream. Make four bursts in the shape of a lilac bloom.

3. Turn the cookie with each petal, creating groups of four. Scatter these over the base to make the lilac blooms stand out.

4. Add pink nonpareils to the center, using tweezers to place them. Continue to pipe the groups of four petals until the flower is filled.

5. Continue to place the nonpareils until each flower cluster has a center.

6. Use green and tip 366 to pipe leaves at the bottom of the lilac. Have the beak facing down and hold the tip ¼ inch off the cookie. Squeeze with a big amount of pressure and slowly pull away to create the long, large lilac leaf. Pipe two or three at the bottom.

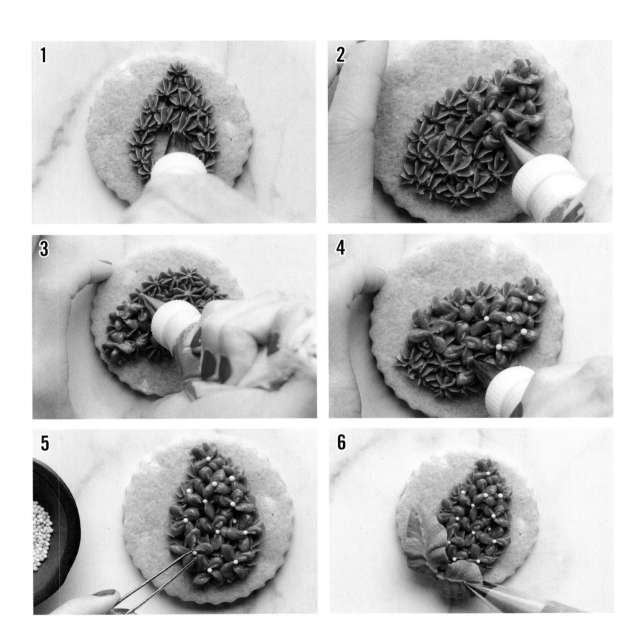

Continued on next page

Hydrangea Instructions

1. With tip 21 and blue buttercream, pipe bursts of buttercream all around the cookie in a circle and fill it in.

2. Attach tip 102 to pipe each little flower. Hold the skinny end away from you and the wide end toward you at the base of the cookie. The piping bag will be angled almost perpendicular with the cookie to let the buttercream flow out flat. Squeeze a small petal, turn the cookie, and pipe a second. Turn the cookie and pipe a third, arranging them like a pinwheel—connected.

3. Pipe the fourth-petal to complete first little flower. Continue this technique until the hydrangea is full of these little flowers.

4. Place purple nonpareils on the center with tweezers.

5. Make more of these four-petal flowers until the base is full.

6. Use moss green buttercream and tip 366. Have the beak facing down and touch the blue buttercream with the end of the tip at the base of the cookie. Use a lot of pressure and let the buttercream billow out, slowly pull away, and then pushing back forward until the leaf is large. Keep pushing and pulling to get ripples.

MASTER TIP

Use the Two-Toned Buttercream technique on page 26 for the hydrangeas to get a slight purple shade in with the blue. Make all different colors of flowers to match whichever lilacs and hydrangeas you prefer.

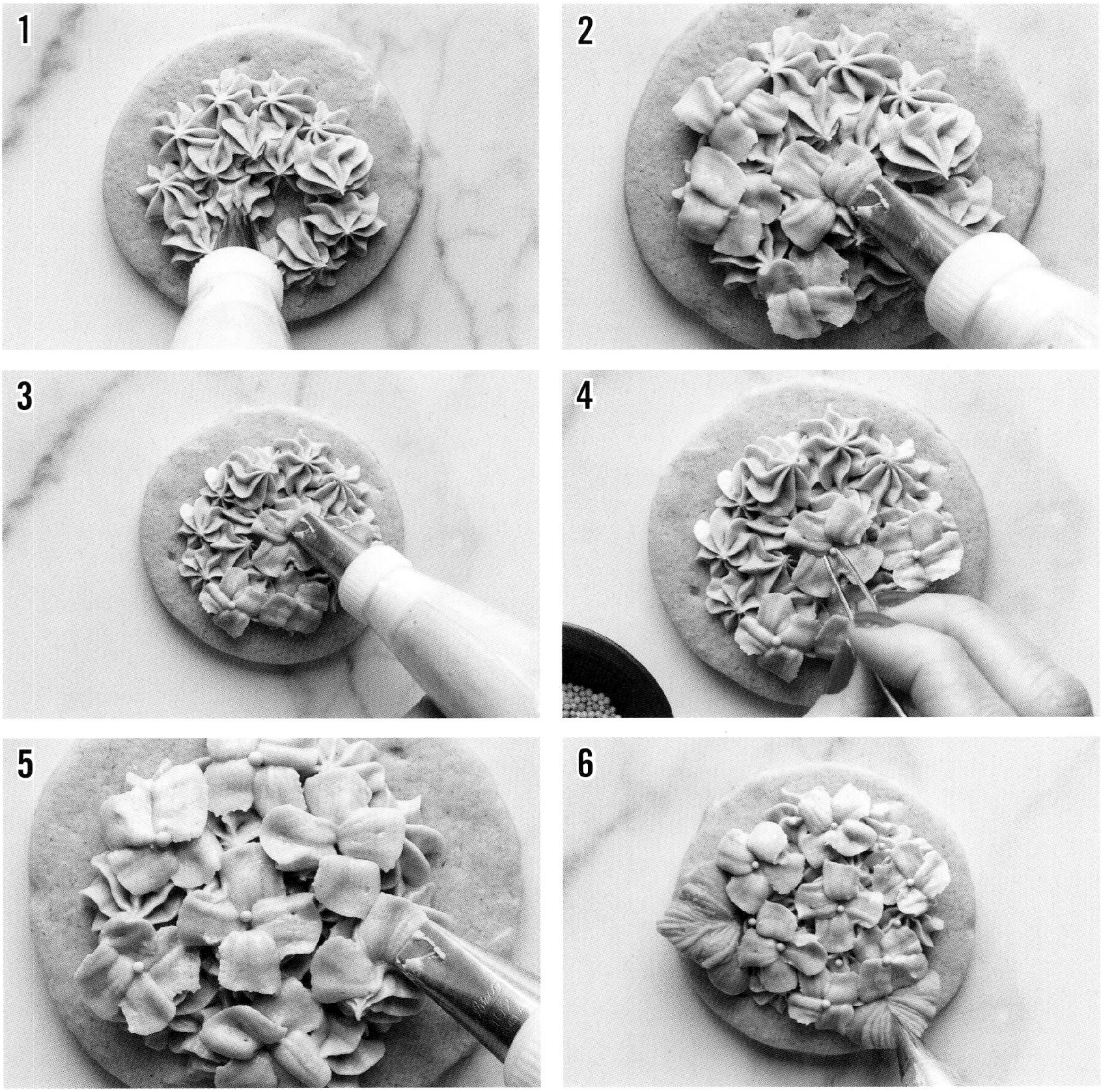
1
2
3
4
5
6

Camillas & Gardenias

It's hard not to be in love with gardenias and camillas. They are beautiful and elegant flowers. I put them together because they look slightly similar but are incredibly different. Gardenias have a special scent that most of us are familiar with. Camillas and gardenias are exquisite flowering shrubs. Let's pipe some!

From the kitchen	**From the drawer**
Round-shaped cookies, 3–4 inches wide Batch of buttercream	Tips 104, 233, and 352 Piping bags Couplers Pink, white, yellow, and green gel food coloring.

Camilla Instructions

1. Use pink buttercream and tip 104. Hold the skinny end of the tip facing away from you and the wide end toward you. Pipe and round your wrist ever so slightly to make each petal. Make five for the bottom base.

2. Move in slightly to pipe the second layer of petals, overlapping the first. Keep piping layers until you have three layers of petals.

3. With yellow and tip 233, pipe one big squeeze right in the center using the grass tip. Pull up while squeezing and then stop and pull up to break the buttercream.

4. Using tip 352 and green buttercream, pipe the leaves. Have the beak facing down and start piping holding the bag almost straight up and down. Squeeze a big amount of buttercream and pull up while angling the bag toward you to get a leaf that's angled up and outward.

Continued on next page

Gardenia Instructions

1. With green buttercream and tip 104, hold the skinny end of the tip facing away from you and the wide end toward you. Pipe two small, rounded leaves at the base of the cookie.

2. Using white buttercream and tip 104, hold the skinny end of the tip facing away from you and the wide end toward you. Pipe and round your wrist ever so slightly to make each petal. Pipe three petals for the first layer in a triangle shape that is spread out.

3. After you pipe the first three, pipe three more petals in the empty space between each one. The first layer of petals will have six.

4. Then start piping smaller petals to build the cookie's center.

5. Start overlapping the petals and pipe where each one leaves off. Slightly overlap to give more of a spiral look to the petals.

6. The center will be small. Pipe the last petal as just a strip of buttercream to complete.

MASTER TIP

Make the camillas bright pink, red, or white. I love these natural shades of colors. Practice on a plate before you pipe on a cookie to get the petals right. This will take practice!

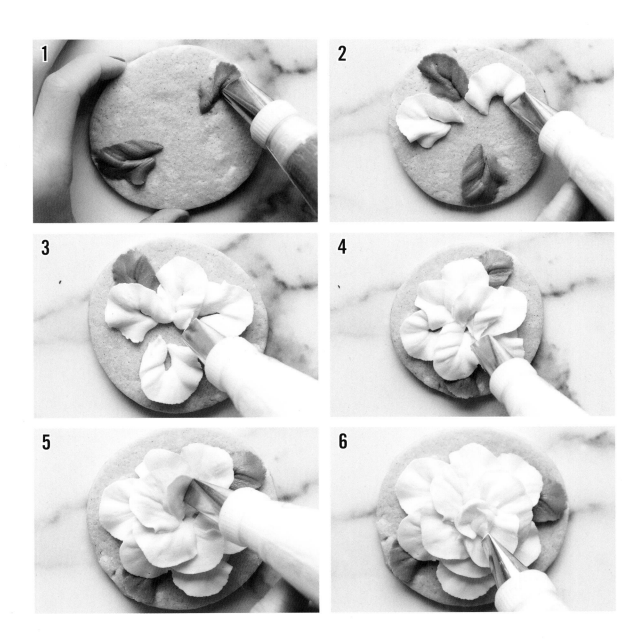

Lilies
page 297

Lilies

We have calla lilies, stargazer lilies, and water lilies. I am such a huge fan of lilies. They are gorgeous, and there are many varieties. I'm so excited to share these because, I have to tell you, I was screaming with joy, feeling victorious, after I frosted these. My sister and I were so excited when I perfectly replicated these in buttercream form.

From the kitchen

Round-shaped cookies, 3–4 inches wide
Batch of buttercream

From the drawer

Tips 104, 125, 4, 363, and 352
Piping bags
Couplers
Pink, purple, white, yellow, orange, and
    green gel food coloring.
Red or deep pink nonpareils
Chocolate jimmies/sprinkles

Calla Lily Instructions

1. With tip 125 and green buttercream, hold the skinny end of the piping tip facing away from you and the wide end toward you at the base of the cookie. Pipe one large leaf with the piping bag tilted at a 45° angle. Squeeze, round up at the tip, and pull downward to pipe the other side of the leaf. To pipe a stem, hold the round, wide end at the very bottom of the cookie and pull upward while squeezing and meet in the middle of the leaf.

2. Now, using purple and tip 125, pipe the back of the lily. Start squeezing with the skinny end facing away from you to get the thin petal. Start on top of the leaf and stem, pipe and pull to the side slightly, then pull up and around to make the first part.

Continued on next page

3. Don't break away from the petal yet. Bring the buttercream over top while turning your wrist all the way over to get the opposite end of the petal to show and bring it downward.

4. Take tip 363 and yellow buttercream and pipe inside of the lily and pull outward to get the center.

Water Lily Instructions

1. Using tip 125 and green buttercream, hold the skinny end away from you and the wide end toward you. Hold the bag perpendicular to the table and the base of the cookie so, when you pipe, the buttercream flows out flat. Start piping almost in the center, pipe and pull straight up, then with a steady stream of buttercream, pipe and turn cookie all the way around. When you're ¾ of the way done, stop, and pipe straight down to make a lily pad.

2. Take light pink mixed with a tiny bit of orange to get a coral color. Use tip 352 and start piping just over the lily pad, with the beak facing down. Squeeze to see the buttercream billow out and pull upward and out to get each long petal of the flower. Create two layers of petals, working your way inward.

3. As you come to the center, pull the piping bag up and then out to get petals that stick up but slightly lay down like the photo. You should be piping at a slight angle toward you.

4. Using tip 4 and yellow buttercream, pipe the center of the lily by squeezing and pulling up until you reach the desired length. Stop squeezing and pull up to break the buttercream.

Continued on next page

Stargazer Lily Instructions

1. Use the Two-Toned Buttercream on page 26 to get the pink strip down the center of the leaf. If the pink is coming out of the skinny end of the tip, adjust it so it flows from the wide end. Hold the skinny end of the piping tip facing away from you and the wide end toward you at the base of the cookie. Using tip, start piping in the middle of the cookie and pull upward, stop at the top, but don't round. Instead, come straight down to get a pointed petal.

2. Make three petals in a triangle. Then pipe the second layer of petals, three more, one in between each petal already piped.

3. Pipe the last of six total petals and bring it in close to the center of the cookie.

4. Sprinkle red or deep pink nonpareils on the center of the petals.

5. With green buttercream and tip 4, start in the center with the piping bag straight up and down. Pipe and gently pull up while still squeezing. Stop where you want the stamen to stop. Pipe a cluster of five or more.

6. Take chocolate jimmies or sprinkles and place one on each end of the stamen using tweezers for accurate placement.

MASTER TIP

Make the petals dark pink for the lilies. These are advanced and tricky, so practice, practice, practice! Use a plate to pipe on before moving to a cookie. You will get it after a few tries, so just keep piping.

"I wake up every day believing that today is going to be better than yesterday." —Will Smith

Celebrations

Lovin' You Cookie Cake

page 306

Elegant Celebration Cookie Cake

page 308

Lovin' You Cookie Cake

We are huge fans of chocolate chip cookies; my son Mikie would eat them every night if he could. So many times, I've caught him staring at the oven, patiently waiting for the cookie to be done. We even turned chocolate chip cookies into mug form on my Instagram together. The warm, delicious, buttery brown sugar taste with the semi-sweet chocolate melted to perfection is like a hug in cookie form. This is similar to my regular chocolate chip cookie recipe but it's adjusted to make one huge cookie. I decorated this very simply and to the point: "Lovin' you, is easy cuz you're beautiful." Find the recipe on page 103.

From the kitchen
Chocolate chip cookie cake
Batch of buttercream

From the drawer
Tips 2 and 1M
Piping bags
Coupler
Pink gel food coloring
Mini chocolate chips
Colored confetti sprinkles

Chocolate Chip Cookie Cake Instructions

1. With tip 2 and bright pink buttercream, pipe on the words LOVIN' YOU by simply squeezing with a steady amount of pressure to pipe each letter. Make sure to mark where the word begins and ends so you don't wind up having words off center to the cake.

2. Take a piping bag, cut off the end about 1 inch, drop down tip 1M, and fill with plain buttercream. Hold the piping tip just off the base of the cookie and have it at a 45° angle on the edge of the cookie cake. Start squeezing and let the buttercream flow out to create a rounded tunnel-looking braid by moving the bag up and around and down to get each loop.

3. Continue to pipe around the border with a steady flow. To turn the cake, simply stop piping and break the buttercream, then move the cake and pick up where you left off.

4. Define the tunnel by doing the same up, down, and around swirl motion, as pictured.

5. The braid will meet where you started. Try to blend it right up to the beginning.

6. Sprinkle on mini chocolate chips and colored confetti to zhoosh it up for the party.

MASTER TIP

The swirl braid is really fun and can be done in any color. Use chocolate buttercream for a beautiful and delicious design.

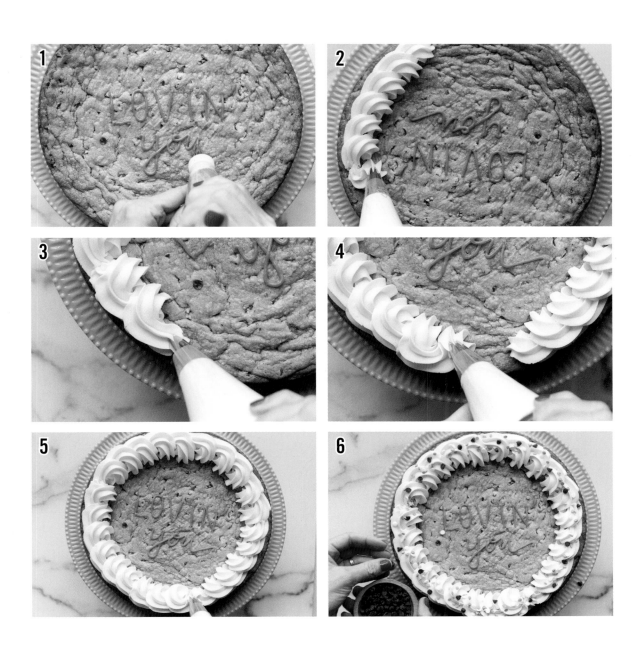

Elegant Celebration Cookie Cake

Sugar cookie cakes are just perfect for anyone who wants to celebrate a birthday, a baptism, a job promotion—just being alive is enough reason to celebrate! Even a Get Well or Sympathy cookie cake will lift someone's heart. Decorate this using any colors, change up the sprinkles to fit any theme. This cookie is tender and delicious with the perfect amount of buttery, salty sweetness. Grab the recipe on page 107.

From the kitchen	From the drawer
Sugar cookie cake	Tip 1M
Batch of buttercream	Piping bag
	Pink gel food coloring

Sugar Cookie Cake Instructions

1. Start with tip 1M. You don't need a coupler; just drop the tip down in the piping bag with the end of the bag cut off, about 1 inch from the bottom. Use pink buttercream and pipe the border of the cookie cake. Hold the piping bag straight up and down, squeeze a large amount of buttercream, and swirl it up and around to the right and then pull down. It's like a swirled teardrop.

2. Now do the same technique but start piping on the tail of the last one. Pipe up and to the left, around, and down.

3. Keep piping around the cake while placing the next one lightly over the tail of the last.

4. You will be squeezing with a large amount of pressure while piping this technique. Stop squeezing as you're pulling down to finish each strand.

5. Continue on around the entire cookie. This design looks similar to rosettes, but they are pulled down instead of ending the rosette in a circle.

6. The very last one will connect the design around the cookie cake.

MASTER TIP

Add on any desired sprinkles or leave plain. Change the color of the border to fit any theme or mood. Make a rainbow for a fun design. Practice this technique on a plate so you feel confident before moving on to the cake.

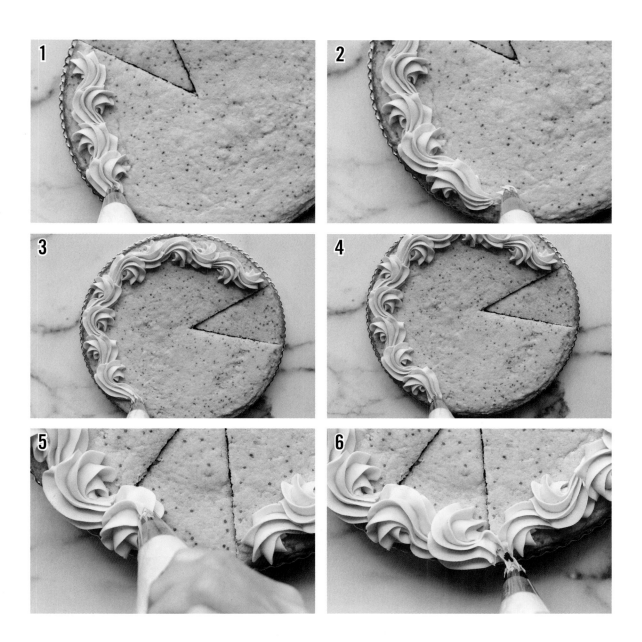

Mother's Day
page 312

Father's Day

page 318

#1 DAD

Mother's Day

Baking is my love language. I bake so much, and for everyone around me, to show them that I care. On Mother's Day, I don't want to bake; I want to relax and get pampered, hence Relaxation Day cookies! I absolutely love to get flowers—flowers make me so happy—so I added a beautiful bouquet in this set. It's funny, because when Mike and I had just started dating, I told him one year that I didn't want anything, which is code for "Honey, buy me flowers." And bless his heart, he didn't get me anything because he really thought I didn't want anything. This is probably the case for some, yes, but not me! Needless to say, flowers arrive on every single holiday now. He's the best husband ever. (I've also since learned to communicate better.)

From the kitchen
Oval-, bouquet-, garland-, and round-shaped cookies
½ batch of buttercream
Batch of flooding buttercream

From the drawer
Tips 102, 352, and 4
Piping bags
Tipless piping bags
Couplers
Scribe or toothpick
Pink, black, white, yellow, and green gel food coloring.

Mom Garland Instructions

1. Take white flood-consistency buttercream and put some in a tipless piping bag. Snip a little off the tip and pipe a line for the garland string. Let dry for 10 minutes. Pipe the banner flags that hang down by outlining and filling it in.

2. Take the scribe tool and make the edges crisp and pointed and swirl out any bumps. Let dry for 10 more minutes.

3. With black, thick, flood-consistency buttercream, pipe M O M, in the center three flags of the banner.

4. With tip 102 and regular pink buttercream, on an empty flag, pipe a small bloom with the skinny end away from you and the wide end toward you at the base of the cookie. Make little bursts of buttercream and round the petals for a delicate little blossom.

5. With tip 4 and yellow buttercream, on the last empty flag, squeeze a large amount of buttercream and then pipe tiny dots on top for a little cluster. Then use tip 352 and light green buttercream, hold the beak facing down, and let the buttercream billow out of the sides and then stop for a small leaf. Add some greenery to the pink bloom on the other flag, if desired.

6. Use the white flood buttercream to pipe small loops on either end of the garland string to complete the cookie.

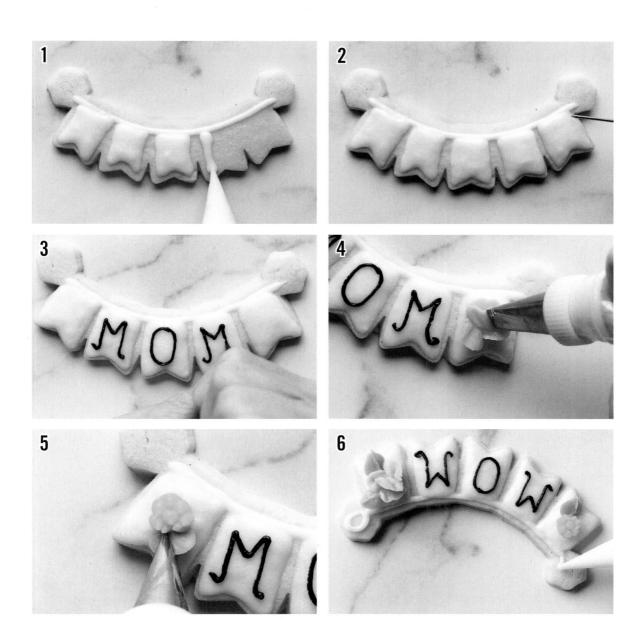

Continued on next page

Cucumber Instructions

1. Using light green flood-consistency buttercream, pipe around a circle cookie and fill it in. Use a scribe tool to make the edges sharp and swirl out any bumps.

2. Take white flood consistency buttercream and pipe five seeds in the center of the cucumber.

Face Mask Instructions

1. Use the Freezer Frosting Method on page 31 and use the same oval shape as the cookie. Make this base any skin color shade. Take white flood-consistency buttercream and pipe a small wavy part on top for the start of the towel on her head.

2. Use green flood consistency buttercream and outline the two eyes rather large, and then outline the mouth and face.

3. Fill in the face for where the face mask would go. You will want a little texture here, so a thicker flood buttercream is great for this.

4. Use pink, thick, flood-consistency buttercream to pipe a heart mouth.

5. Use black, thick, flood-consistency buttercream to pipe eyelashes in the eye holes.

6. Then pipe a swoop of the towel, covering the face a little. Piping in this order makes the towel stand off a little to provide volume—closer to what a towel really looks like.

MASTER TIP

Make these cookies any color for Mom. Make sure to make the eye holes and mouth to the face mask large because, when you fill it in, the buttercream settles and can close the circle for the eyes if you're not careful. Make sure the tip for the flowers is facing the right direction, the wide end up will make a blob of a flower. Practice on a plate if you're not used to the petal tip. Keep flooding buttercream warm by reheating it in the microwave at 3- to 4-second intervals. It will melt and become useless if it's overheated.

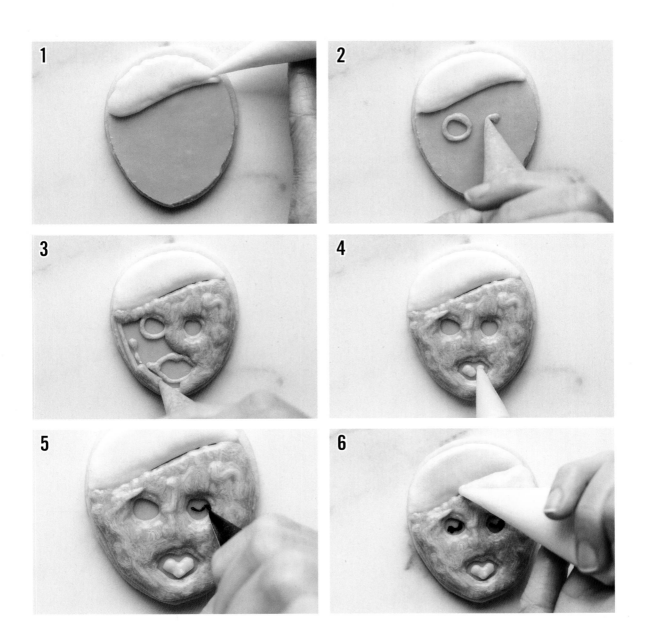

Continued on next page

Bouquet Instructions

1. With white flood-consistency buttercream, pipe the vase. Use a scribe tool to make the edges straight and crisp. Swirl out any bumps.

2. Using pink regular buttercream and tip 102, hold the skinny end facing up and away from you and the wide end down and toward you. Pipe around, squeezing with a steady stream of pressure, and pipe the bottom row of petals. Pipe with gentle up and down motions to get ruffles. Pipe a second row smaller for the center. Then frost one last petal down the middle for a pink carnation.

3. Use tip 102 and white buttercream to pipe a side view of a bloom. Pipe one line, starting another layer where one end stops. Overlap and layer until you have a small side view.

4. Next, use peach buttercream by mixing a little pink with yellow this time. Use tip 102, with the skinny end again facing away from you. Pipe small rows of long petals for a little side-view blossom.

5. With yellow buttercream and tip 4, pipe a small mound of buttercream and then cover it with tiny dots or bursts of buttercream. This is a little filler flower for texture and color.

6. Finally, take light green buttercream with tip 352 and, with the beak pointed down, squeeze a large amount of buttercream and pull back, then stop and pull away further to break the buttercream. Continue adding greenery to fill the bouquet by repeating this technique.

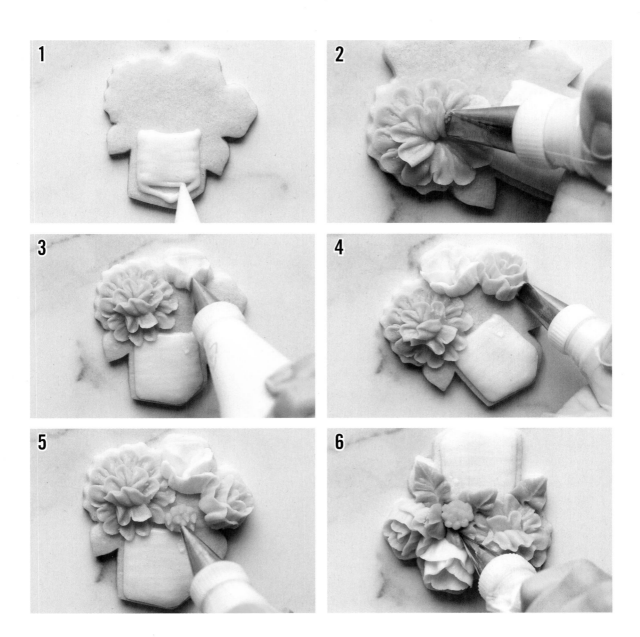

Father's Day

We love Mike so much; Father's Day is the perfect day to make sure he knows just how much we appreciate him. If you know my husband, you know he is a dessert lover, and that's why our marriage works so well! Baking is my love language, and eating baked goods is his. I love his sweet tooth. Mike also has a love for his lawn, so lawnmower cookies just suit him. Let's mow these cookies and kick some grass, shall we?

From the kitchen	**From the drawer**
Square- and present-shaped cookies	Tips 47, 48, 233, 352, 12, 2, and 4
Batch of buttercream	Piping bags
	Couplers
	Red, black, white, yellow, blue, brown, and green gel food coloring.
	Offset spatula
	White nonpareils

Lawn Mower Instructions

1. Using an offset spatula, spread a small amount of light blue buttercream on the top half of the cookie for the sky. You can also leave it plain.

2. Take green buttercream with grass tip 233, and pipe a strip of buttercream down across the bottom of the cookie.

3. Using Ateco tip 47 and red buttercream, have the smooth end of the tip facing up and pipe a line of buttercream in the middle of the cookie. Pipe a second strip of buttercream but make it curved so it looks like a lawn mower.

4. Use black buttercream with tip 12 attached. Hold piping bag ¼ inch off the cookie, holding the bag straight up and down, squeeze, and make a closed circle. Make a large one for the back tire and a smaller one for the front tire.

5. Attach tip 4 to the black buttercream. Turn the cookie upside down and pipe the handle bar coming from the tire and also from the red part of the lawn mower. Pipe a black top right on the center of the red body for the engine that pops up.

6. Take the grass tip 233 again with the green buttercream and make grass coming from the front of the lawn mower, as if the grass hasn't been mowed there yet. Squeeze and pull up and then stop piping to break the buttercream.

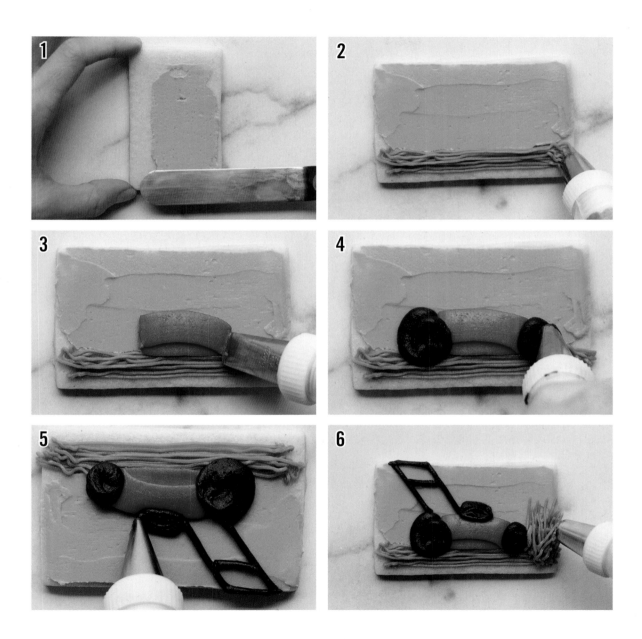

Continued on next page

TV Instructions

1. Pipe black buttercream using tip 12 onto the gift-shaped cookie, and then use an offset spatula to smooth it out for the screen of the TV.

2. Attach tip 4 and pipe two bunny ears coming from the TV.

3. Use Wilton tip 48 and gray buttercream, and pipe using the flat side facing upward. Hold the piping bag almost perpendicular with the table and base of cookie for a flat stream of buttercream. Pipe a border around the TV screen. Pipe the two horizontal sides first and then the vertical sides of the TV.

4. Use yellow and tip 4, and hold the piping bag straight up and down for a flat flow of buttercream. Pipe a large M on the right side of the TV screen. Then use tip 2 and red buttercream, and pipe TV on top of the large M.

Gift Instructions

1. Using blue buttercream and tip 4, outline the present and fill it in back and forth. Hold piping bag at a 45° angle so the buttercream flows out like a tube of toothpaste. Sprinkle some white nonpareils onto the present.

2. Use gray buttercream with tip 4 attached and pipe the ribbon. Pipe longways and then vertically and meet in the middle, but off center, a little like a present. Make a design on top by adding a couple loops to the bow.

MASTER TIP

Make black buttercream by using the Chocolate Cream Cheese Frosting on page 131. Add a little black to it and it will color nicely. Cover buttercream with plastic wrap and let the color deepen overnight on the counter.

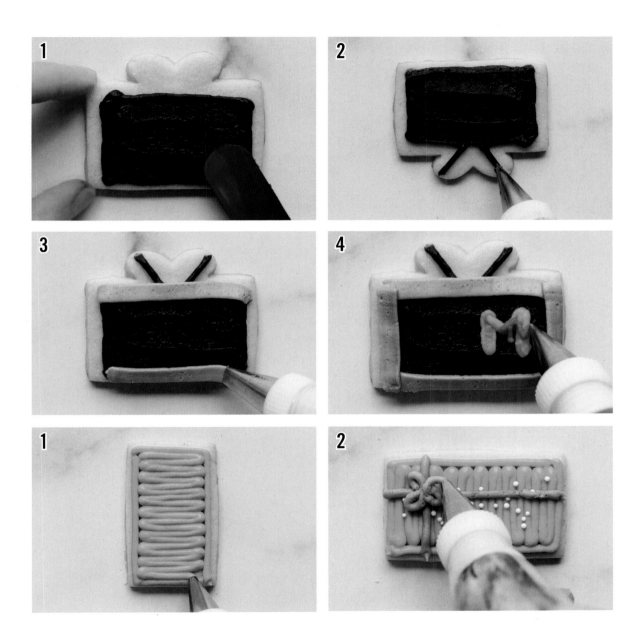

Continued on next page

BBQ Instructions

1. Use black buttercream and tip 12 and make dollops of buttercream on the top of a rectangle cookie for the BBQ charcoal briquets. Don't pipe on the very edge. We will add a grill.

2. With gray buttercream and tip 4, pipe the grill across the charcoal. Make the space in-between small like a grill on a BBQ.

3. To the gray buttercream, attach tip 47 with the flat side upward, and pipe a border around for the grill edge. Pipe longways first and then both sides.

4. With brown buttercream and tip 12, hold piping bag straight up and down and pipe dollops of buttercream. Twist off the end instead of pulling straight up for the hamburger patties. Make four to five patties.

5. Next, take a lighter color of brown buttercream, mix in a tiny bit of red, and attach tip 4. Hold the piping bag angled at 45° so the buttercream flows out like a tube of toothpaste, and pipe hotdogs on the other side of the grill.

6. Finally, use tip 2 and black buttercream and pipe charred marks in the burgers and hotdogs.

1

2

3

4

5

6

Cats
page 325

Cats

You all loved the dogs in the first book so much and have been asking for cat cookies, so I'm very excited to share these. I had an orange kitty growing up that I named Corky. I loved him so much that I named two more cats after him. I've had lots of Corkys! I made a Siamese cat after my friend Kristin's beautiful baby she posts about on Instagram—I just had to make her kitty into a delicious cookie. My sister loves gray kitties, so naturally we needed to add one in to make a fabulous clowder!

From the kitchen
Round- and cat face–shaped cookies
Batch of buttercream

From the drawer
Tips 233 and 2
Piping bags
Couplers
Pink, purple, black, white, blue, green, and orange gel food coloring
Heart sprinkles
Mini marshmallows
Food-safe paintbrush

Yarn Instructions

1. Using pink buttercream and tip 233, pipe around in a circle from the outside, piping in.
2. Pipe some yarn-looking pieces across the cookie one way, and then pipe over a different direction so it looks like a ball of yarn.

Continued on next page

Tabby Instructions

1. Take mini marshmallows and flatten them longways. Cut into a kite shape by trimming the top corners and bottom corners with scissors. You will need two marshmallows per cookie. Paint the marshmallow with watered-down green gel food coloring. If you don't water it down, it will be too dark.

2. Using tip 233 and light orange buttercream, cover the base of the cookie in buttercream—just pipe it on. Pick up and gently drop the cookie down on the table to settle the buttercream.

3. Holding the piping bag straight up and down, pipe fur all over the face of the cookie. Squeeze and release all the way around.

4. Squeeze a large amount of buttercream for the bridge of the nose to build it up so it stands out.

5. Next, pipe two cheeks under the nose at the bottom of the cookie on either side to make it look puffy. Take a darker orange buttercream and tip 233 and pipe two strips of buttercream at the top of the cookie.

6. Then, using tip 2 and white buttercream, pipe on whiskers, starting at the cheeks. Keep piping and pulling toward the outside of the cookie. Make three on either side. Pipe a small mouth under the nose and between the cheeks we built up.

7. Use tweezers to place the eyes on the cat's face. Be very careful with placement; it can change the look of the cat's face. Place the heart under the bridge of the nose.

8. Use tip 2 and black buttercream to pipe big, round eyeballs on each eye.

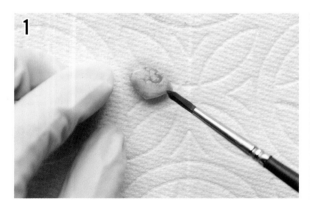

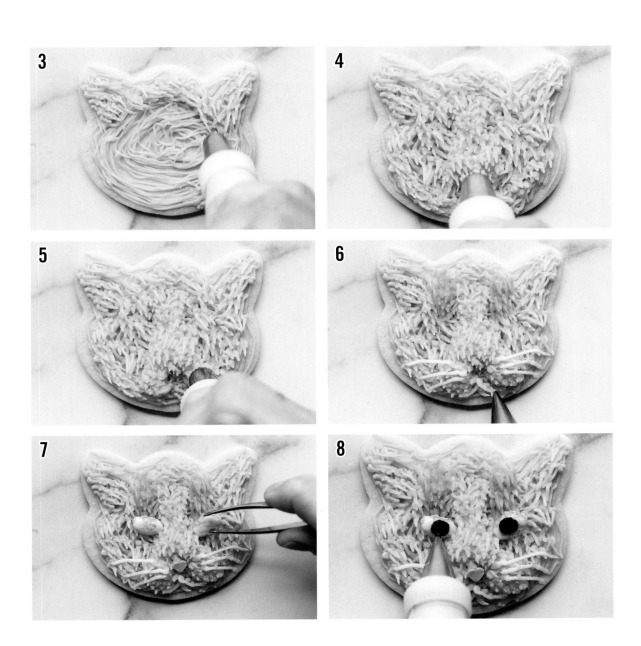

Continued on next page

Siamese Instructions

1. Take mini marshmallows and flatten longways. Cut into a kite shape by trimming the top corners and bottom corners with scissors. You will need two marshmallows per cookie. Paint on the marshmallow with watered down blue gel food coloring. If you don't water it down, it will be too dark. Using tip 233 and white buttercream, cover the base of the cookie in buttercream. Just pipe it on, but leave the ears unfrosted at this time. Pick up and gently drop the cookie down on the table to settle the buttercream. Pipe two cheeks at the bottom of the cookie on either side to make it look puffy.

2. Use black buttercream with tip 233 and squeeze a large amount of buttercream for the bridge of the nose to build it up so it stands out.

3. Using black again, pipe above the cheeks where the eyes will go, and pipe a little black for the mouth, as well.

4. Using black again, pipe the cat's ears.

5. With gray buttercream and tip 233, pipe around the black on the face to blend in the black fur to the white fur. Pipe in your cat's markings if they are a little different than pictured.

6. Take white buttercream and attach tip 2. Pipe whiskers that come from the cheeks and go out to the edge of the cookie. Pipe three per side. Pipe a small mouth under the nose bridge that we built up.

7. Use tweezers to place the eyes on the cat's face. Be very careful with placement; it can change the look of the cat's face. Place the heart nose just under the bridge. Use tweezers for this, as well.

8. Use tip 2 and black buttercream to pipe big, round eyeballs on each eye.

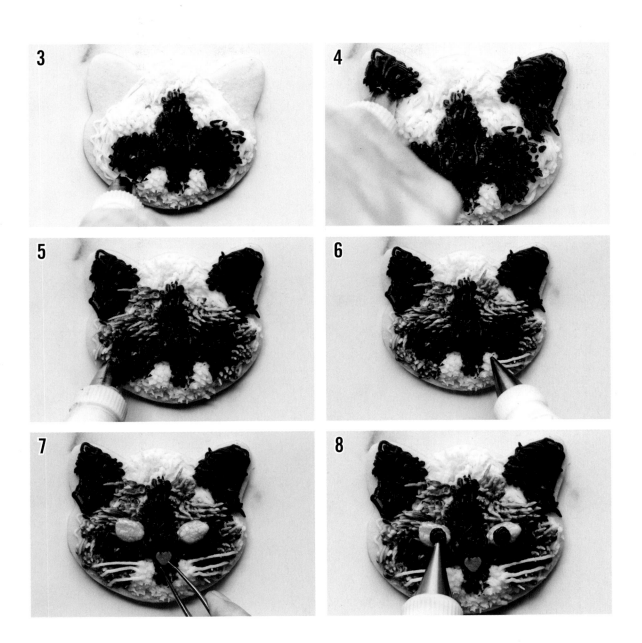

Continued on next page

Russian Blue Instructions

1. Take mini marshmallows and flatten longways. Cut into a kite shape by trimming the top corners and bottom corners with scissors. You will need two marshmallows per cookie. Paint on the marshmallow with watered down green gel food coloring. If you don't water it down, it will be too dark. Using tip 233 and gray buttercream, cover the base of the cookie in buttercream—just pipe it on. Pick up and gently drop the cookie down on the table to settle the buttercream.

2. Then hold the piping bag straight up and down and pipe fur all over the face of the cookie. Squeeze and release all the way around.

3. Squeeze a large amount of buttercream for the bridge of the nose to build it up so it stands out. Next, pipe two cheeks under the nose at the bottom of the cookie on either side to make it look puffy.

4. Use tweezers to place the eyes on the cat's face. Be very careful with placement; it can change the look of the cat's face. Place the heart nose on, as well.

5. Using tip 2 and white buttercream, pipe on whiskers starting at the cheeks, and then keep piping and pulling toward the outside of the cookie. Make three on either side. Pipe a small mouth under the nose and between the cheeks we built up.

6. Use tip 2 and black buttercream to pipe big, round eyeballs on each eye.

MASTER TIP

Make sure to build up the nose and the cheeks to make it look like a cat's face—this is very important. The eye placement is very important, also—angle them to look like cat eyes.

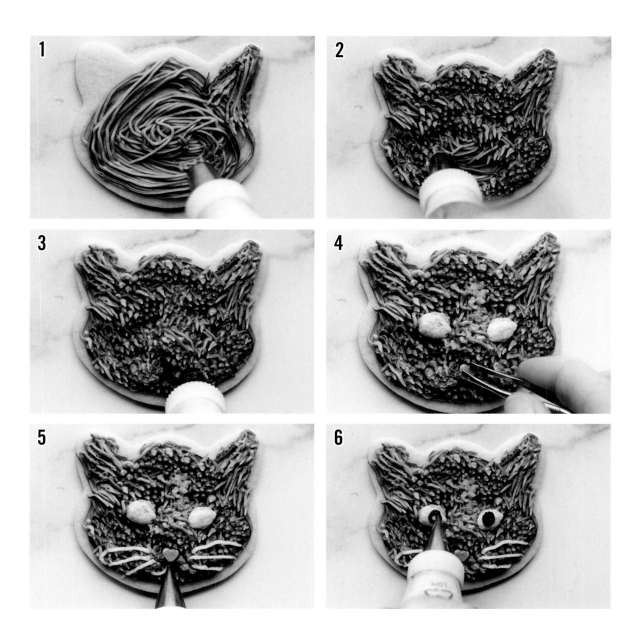

Bonus

Orchid Flower

Orchids are exotic and beautiful. Make them deep purple for a bright and beautiful cookie. This cookie was made and graced the cover of the book; it should have had its own cookie plate because it's that beautiful, but I'm glad you'll still make them. Add them to any cookie plate.

From the kitchen
Round-shaped cookies
Batch of buttercream

From the drawer
Tips 125 and 81
Piping bags
Couplers
White and yellow gel food coloring.
Purple nonpareils

Orchid Instructions

1. Use tip 125 and white buttercream. Have the skinny end of the tip away from you at the edge of the cookie and the wide end at the base of the cookie. Start piping the bottom two petals.

2. Next, pipe the third top petal. This will be bigger so squeeze a larger amount of buttercream. Round your wrist ever so slightly.

3. Pipe two smaller petals right on top of the top large petal.

4. Using yellow buttercream and tip 81, hold the piping bag straight up and down and slightly angled to the right. Pipe the right middle side of the stamen. Then pipe the left side by facing the tip to the opposite side, then squeeze, pull up, and stop squeezing and pull away to break the buttercream.

5. Finally, pipe one middle part on the bottom so it looks like a U. Pipe and pull up and out, stop squeezing, and pull away to break the buttercream.

6. Sprinkle the purple nonpareils in the center of the orchid.

MASTER TIP

These petals are tricky and it's very important to pipe them as pictured. The placement is very important to make it look like an orchid. Practice on a plate before you move to a cookie.

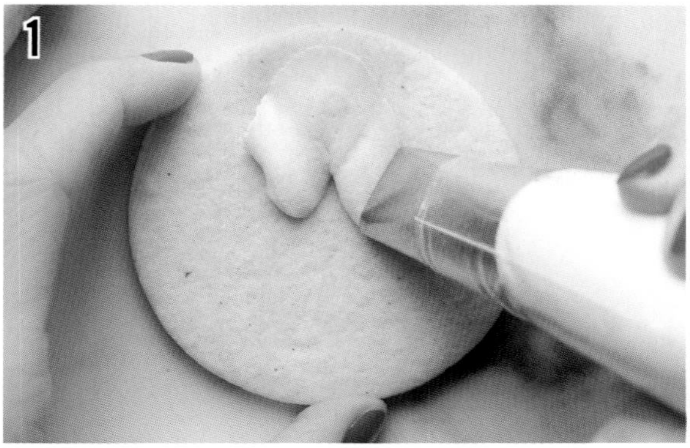
1

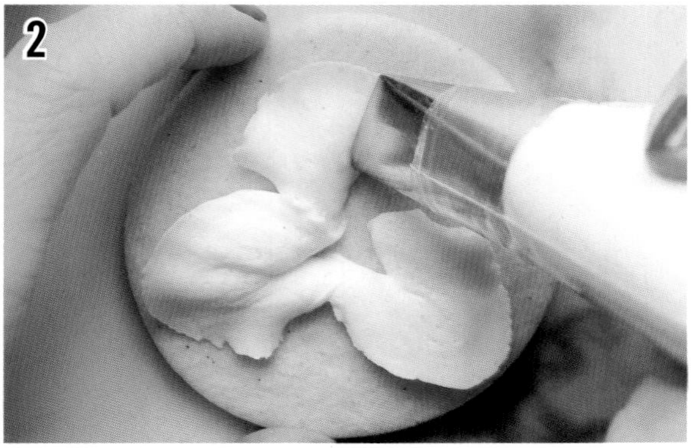
2

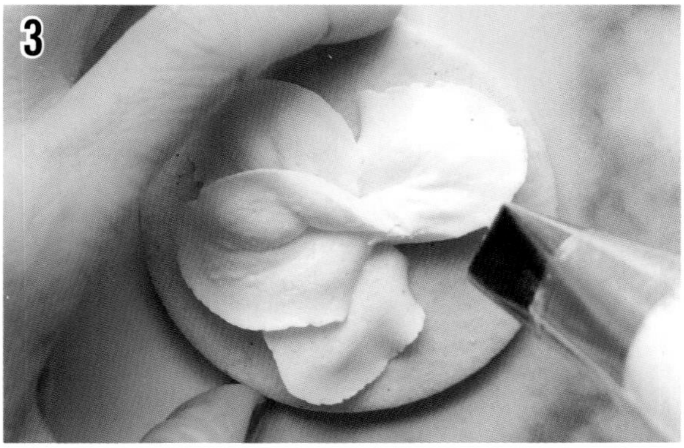
3

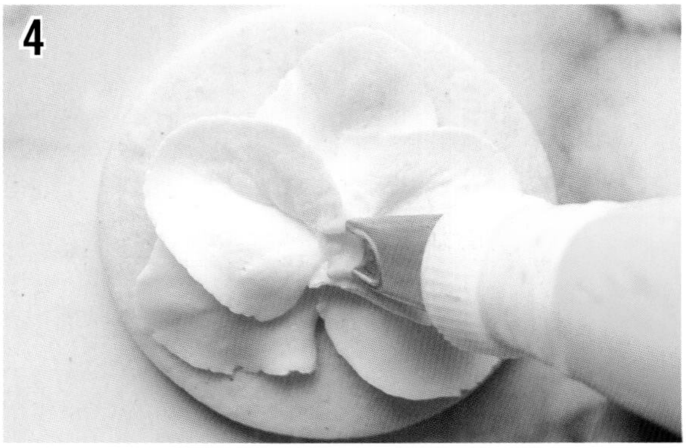
4

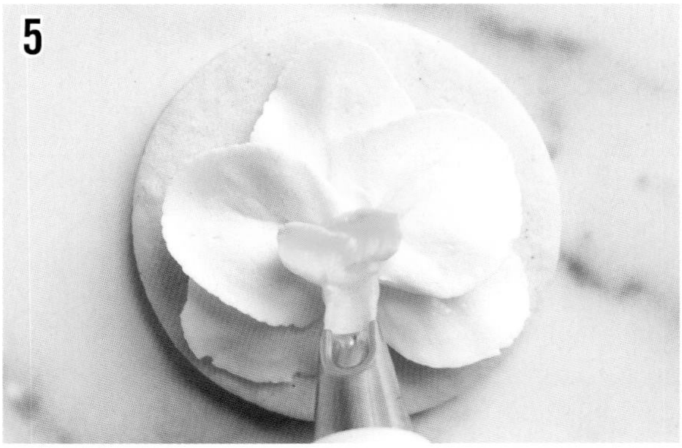
5

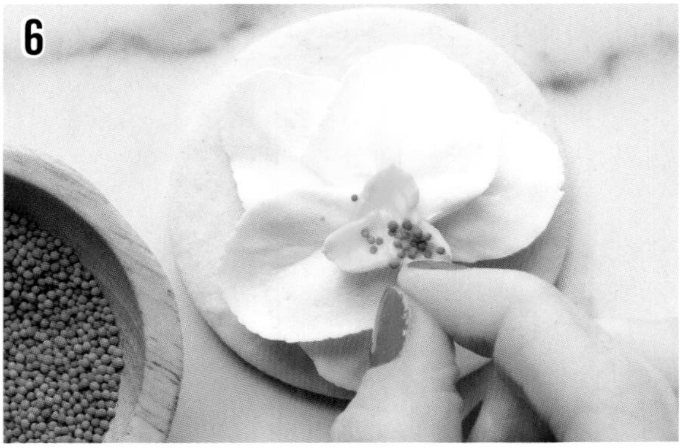
6

Fall Pumpkin Basket

This basket of pumpkins is so fun and festive—great for any harvest party theme. Make the pumpkins any color to add to the beauty.

From the kitchen	**From the drawer**
Cupcake-shaped cookies	Tips 21, 32, 18, and 12
Batch of buttercream	Piping bags
	Tipless piping bags
	Couplers
	White, orange, green, and brown gel food coloring.

Basket Instructions

1. Use brown flood-consistency buttercream and make strips on the bottom of the basket but leave a little space between each one. Let dry for 15 minutes.

2. Pipe two lines horizontally across the wood strips.

3. With green buttercream and tip 32, pipe holding the bag straight up and down, pulling inward with each part of the pumpkin.

4. Next, use orange buttercream and tip 21, and pipe the same way but larger. Starting outside, pipe and pull in with each section of the pumpkin. Attach tip 12 and make a dollop of buttercream for around pumpkin.

5. Use white buttercream with tip 12 and pipe more pumpkins by making large dollops of buttercream.

6. Finally, use tip 18 and pipe stems in the center of each pumpkin.

MASTER TIPS

Make the pumpkins pastel or all orange but just different shades. Change it up and make them apples using the large round tip 12 and then make small stems and leaves for autumn.

Cut the top of the cupcake cookie off to make it flatter if you don't want the cupcake point on these cookies. I found that frozen cookies need to be thawed completely before frosting with flood buttercream because the cookie defrosts and makes the buttercream run together. The extra condensation isn't good for these.

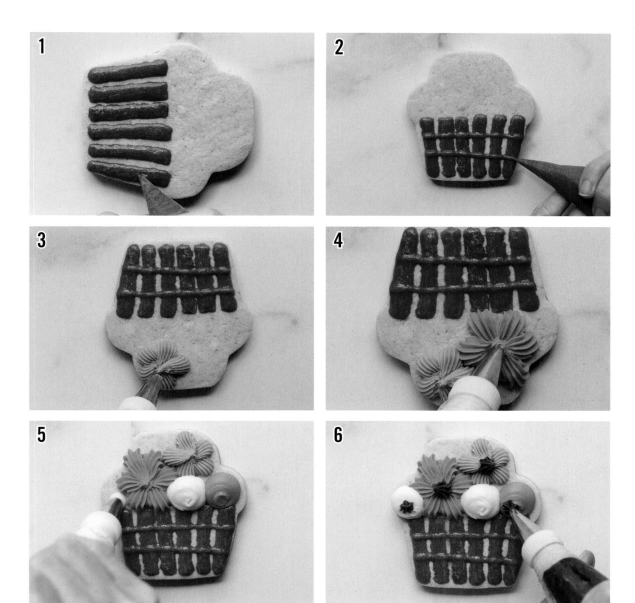

Sunflower

I wanted to make a versatile flower that can be used in multiple colors to make different flowers. Simple and beautiful.

From the kitchen
Round-shaped cookies
Batch of buttercream

From the drawer
Tips 104 and 18
Piping bags
Couplers
Yellow and brown gel food coloring.

Sunflower Instructions

1. With tip 104 and yellow buttercream, pipe with the skinny end facing away from you and the wide end toward you at the base of the cookie. Start piping on the edge but leave a little space to turn the cookie with your fingers. With a steady stream, pipe and move up and down with the piping bag to make small petals.

2. Pipe a second layer just under the first to work your way inward. Continue in a steady stream of buttercream.

3. For the center, use brown and tip 18. Hold the piping bag straight up and down while squeezing bursts of buttercream to fill the center disk of the sunflower. Squeeze and release all the way until it's filled.

MASTER TIP

Make these white and yellow for a daisy. Make the center smaller for a brown-eyed Susan.

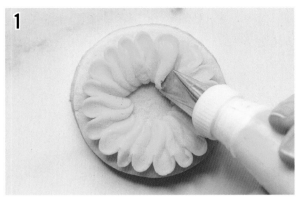

Acknowledgments

Mike

You and the kids are everything to me—by everything, I really mean everything. My cookie pusher, my best friend, and my biggest fan. You love sweets more than anyone I know, which is very endearing. I always develop recipes with you in mind. When I didn't think I could finish this book, you helped me believe in myself and you always remind me how big God is. You speak against every doubt I have ever had. You're always ready for our next adventure. There is no one on the planet I'd rather be doing this beautiful, crazy, wild ride with than you. I really love our life, and it's a dream come true to be able to build it together. At the end of my life, my relationships with you and the kids will ultimately be my greatest accomplishments. I would never take anything we have for granted, and I know how blessed we are. We are an amazing team, and as long as we have each other, we have everything we need. Thank you for being strong enough to hold me up but gentle enough to care for my heart. I love you forever and always, my sweeter than sweet husband.

Reese

My beautiful daughter, my friend. Wow, where do I start? You became an adult and my most special friend in the world. I can always count on you, no questions asked. You show up and surprise me; you are my angel. You're the first person I call about anything exciting (shhhh, don't tell dad and Nonie!). You are the one who cheers the loudest—"YEAHH, MOM!!!!"—I can hear it now. You mean more to me than you can imagine. I can't thank you enough for loving me, supporting me, believing in me, and encouraging me. I really do live for our Facetime calls, our GIF convos, and our dances in the car. You are my breath of fresh air that centers my heart and my brain. I feel like you've been by my side through this whole book, because even though you're not home, you're still here. You really understand me, my heart, and my journey. You support my work and my mission with The Hutch Oven. Thank you for being with me through this. I love the texting in all CAPS when I send you shots of new cookies; it makes me laugh out loud and I get so excited. Thank you for laughing with me and crying with me, especially in this season of writing. You're everything I could hope for in a daughter and a friend. Our relationship and bond are one of my best and greatest treasures in my life. You brighten up my days. We are seriously the same person, haha, but you already knew I'd say that. I love you more, Reesie! You are everything! How the heck are you so amazing?! I'm seriously obsessed with you!

Nick

My guy who will eat all the cookies I make and never get sick of them. I love that you will step in to help when I need you—you're such a good whisker. Thank you for your brutal honesty when I didn't quite nail a recipe that maybe needs a little more work. I like that with that honesty, you are careful with my feelings. Thank you for encouraging me and for telling me I'm doing a good job. Thank you for loving all my cookie designs and for even being excited over the new flower ones. I love showing you what's new because you care about my work and you're always happy for me. I wish I could talk you into more videos and for you to be on camera because I think you have something really special inside of you that the world needs to see. Thanks for cheering on your mama and for being a big support bts. I see you, Nick. I love how close we are, and I wouldn't trade our relationship for anything. Thank you for hugging me for five minutes and waiting for me to let go first when I've had a rough day or I'm at a road block with my work. I'm still going to keep begging you to let me bring you to the set of a show I film. ;) I'm so dang proud to be your mom. You are a one-of-a-kind country boy with a huge heart and one of the best people I know. I love you so much, buddy!

Mikie

My Hollywood boy! You are my light and my loud clapper. My Cookie Monster, it makes me so happy that you love all the desserts I bake. Sharing that part of my life with you is the greatest gift. I love that you are always ready for a cookie video and that you love spending time in the kitchen with me. Thank you for being understanding through this last year and for caring about my work. You are always interested in knowing more and learning what I know. You're so excited for me, and you never miss a thing. I love that you're my baking buddy. (So many people have requested more of our Mikie and me videos!) You are so good to your mama; your kindness has gotten me through long days of working on this book. Thank you for the extra snuggles and for the big kisses every morning. You really get excited over my videos and what I do; you know everything I've created because you care. You even have the first book displayed in your room—I'm so unbelievably honored. Your support fills my soul. Mikie, love of my life, you have my heart. Thank you for being my son and for being proud that I'm your mom. Every time I look at you, I see God's promises. You bring me so much joy! I'm so lucky to have you.

I love you (squeezing your hand in our secret language).

My sister, Jo

Jo Jo, where do I start? Oh my gosh, sister, I'm thinking back to our weekly dates while shooting this book. The screams of excitement and the laughter. AAAHHHHHHHH!! You're one of my biggest cheerleaders and you always say, "You can do it! I couldn't do it. I don't know how you're going to do it, but you always do!" That gave me more confidence than you know. It helped me push through the last month of shooting. I'm truly so thankful for you and that you helped me when my brain was blocked. Thank you for brainstorming with me and for being a truth-teller. Thank you for being an amazing sister and friend. Thank you for helping me believe in myself and pushing me toward my dreams. You help me realize I can do anything. I love your ideas and advice. I had the time of my life doing this with you. I'm thankful for the memories we have shared while shooting this. Gosh, that was fun. We did it, sis!! I love you so much. I'm thankful for you, and I appreciate you.

My sister, Ali

Gertie, I'm so thankful for your encouraging texts and phone calls when I was struggling with exhaustion. Thank you for pushing me forward and for reminding me of how strong I am. I love you so much, and I'm so thankful for you and your support. Thank you for always being here for me and being up for anything. You're my person and one of my biggest fans. I wouldn't have the confidence to do what I do

without you. You always help me see who I can be when I have doubts about myself. When you look at me and remind me of what I'm capable of, I believe in myself. You're my hype girl. That is a huge gift. I can't thank you enough for the big role you play in my life. You're the best sister and the best friend. I love you, Wyatt! "Say when!" Love, Doc.

My sister, Patti

I love you so, so very much. I love how happy you are for me and for how much you support me and the kids. I am so blessed by you and your love for us. We are so thankful for you. Thank you for being my sister, friend, and cheerleader. I love when your eyes light up with joy for things happening in my life. Thank you for really caring, for always watching my segments, buying my books, and for being proud to be my sister and my friend. You're an angel, and I love you so much.

Mom

Dedicating the book wasn't enough. I needed to tell you I love you again, Ma mA. I love you!!

Dad

Thank you for giving me the gift of supporting me through this exciting time in my life. The texts and calls have made me so happy and loved. Thank you for watching every segment and show. Thank you for knowing and remembering what I've cooked and decorated on each segment. Thank you for being proud of my work and telling everyone about my cookies. It means so much. I love you, Dad.

Pop Pop

Thank you for being such a big support for me throughout my life. Thank you for watching all my segments, reading the magazine, loving the first book, and for being the best Pop Pop in the world. I have always strived to make you proud; I know you are proud of me. You have supported me when I've fallen and supported me when I've soared. Thank you, Pop Pop. I love you more than words can say.

Aunt Celia

Thank you for being the baker I look up to. Thank you for supporting me and supporting this book. Thank you for supporting and encouraging my relationship with the Lord. Most of all, thank you for sharing treasured recipes with me and trusting me with them. I love you, Auntie.

Friends!

So many friends have influenced me, given me strength and determination to see this second book through. **Julianna, Abby, Nicole, Kala, Megan, and Christina,** the prayers and constant support have lifted me high. Thank you for always turning me toward Jesus and for helping me through this season of writing. Thank you for knowing my heart and for helping me believe in myself. Thank you for showing up, having my back, and for being the loudest cheerers in the room. Thank you for the "How are you? How's the book coming?" texts and calls. You each play a pivotal and important role in my life and in my work. None of this would mean anything without you. I love each of you deeply. I feel seen by you. **AC:** freezer frost method credit! Thank you, friend, for the ideas! **Chelsea, Kacee, Gentree:** I couldn't have gotten through this without each of you—the High, the laughs, the sweat and the tears. I love you, girls. **Heather:** I can't thank you enough for every time you asked how things were going. Every prayer, every hug, and every text made a huge difference in my work and in my life. The workouts, laughs, tears, and the time have truly been gifts and a light to my soul. Thank you for supporting me in all I do. Thank you for caring so much about my work and for always pointing to God's word and praying over my life. I love you, my friend. **Hannah:** Thank you for the time and for the help on this book, too. Thank you for being a forever friend and for being a special part of my life. You're brilliant and so talented. I'm so lucky to have you. I love you.

My editor, Nicole Frail

I can't thank you enough for believing in me, showing me grace, and for being beside me while doing a second book. I'm so proud of what we have done, and I'm thankful for all of your hard work and input. Thank you for caring so much about this book and for your tireless efforts to make everything perfect. You're the best!

About the Author

Emily Hutchinson, the creator of The Hutch Oven, has built a brand around creative ways to decorate beautiful and achievable buttercream-frosted cookie designs with trusted recipes. She passionately shares her gift of baking, along with her inspiring journey after her daughter passed away from SIDS in 2008. Her heartfelt stories will leave you full of hope and the feel of a warm embrace as you soak up valuable cookie knowledge. Emily is real and relatable, and it's like you're baking right alongside her.

Emily is an authority in her field as a self-taught, avid home baker and decorator. Emily teaches her tips and techniques on national television and in her tutorials. She was the regular cookie decorator on Hallmark's *Home and Family* show (before the show ended) and she landed a seat as one of two judges on Hallmark Drama's *Christmas Cookie Matchup*. Her cookies have been featured on the cover of the holiday collector's edition of *Bake from Scratch* magazine. She works closely with brands like Williams Sonoma. She shares her expertise and inspires many listeners on podcasts and radio stations. Emily has taught numerous celebrities to decorate her creative cookies, such as Lance Bass and Candace Nelson. You can also find Emily on *The Rachael Ray Show* and locally in Seattle, spreading sweetness on the TV screen.

Emily resides in Arlington, Washington, with her husband Mike and three children, Reese, Nick and Mikie. Emily cares about her community, her family and friends, and her church. If Emily isn't in the kitchen baking or recipe testing, you'll find her hanging out with her family or working out at the gym doing HighFitness. Emily and her family have a strong faith; they love Jesus and they love people. Teaching her skills on her large platform has helped her connect with so many and spread joy and hope through her powerful story.

Matthew 5:14 You are the light of the world. A town built on a hill cannot be hidden.

Index

Conversion Charts

Metric and Imperial Conversions

(These conversions are rounded for convenience. Please see recipe for author-provided gram measurements.)

Ingredient	Cups/Tablespoons/ Teaspoons	Ounces
Butter	1 cup/ 16 tablespoons/ 2 sticks	8 ounces
Cheese, shredded	1 cup	4 ounces
Cream cheese	1 tablespoon	0.5 ounce
Cornstarch	1 tablespoon	0.3 ounce
Flour, all-purpose	1 cup/1 tablespoon	4.5 ounces/0.3 ounce
Flour, whole wheat	1 cup	4 ounces
Fruit, dried	1 cup	4 ounces
Fruits or veggies, chopped	1 cup	5 to 7 ounces
Fruits or veggies, pureed	1 cup	8.5 ounces
Honey, maple syrup, or corn syrup	1 tablespoon	0.75 ounce
Liquids: cream, milk, water, or juice	1 cup	8 fluid ounces
Oats	1 cup	5.5 ounces
Salt	1 teaspoon	0.2 ounce
Spices: cinnamon, cloves, ginger, or nutmeg (ground)	1 teaspoon	0.2 ounce
Sugar, brown, firmly packed	1 cup	7 ounces
Sugar, white	1 cup/1 tablespoon	7 ounces/0.5 ounce
Vanilla extract	1 teaspoon	0.2 ounce

Oven Temperatures

Fahrenheit	Celsius	Gas Mark
225°	110°	¼
250°	120°	½
275°	140°	1
300°	150°	2
325°	160°	3
350°	180°	4
375°	190°	5
400°	200°	6
425°	220°	7
450°	230°	8

Altitude Adjustments

	At 3,000 feet	At 5,000 feet	At 7,000 feet
Baking Powder/Soda Per teaspoon	Reduce by ⅛ teaspoon	Reduce by ⅛–¼ teaspoon	Reduce by ¼ teaspoon
Flour Per cup	Add 0–1 tablespoon	Add 0–2 tablespoons	Add 2–4 tablespoons
Sugar Per cup	Reduce by 0–1 tablespoon	Reduce by 0–2 tablespoons	Reduce by 1–3 tablespoons

Author's Note: Recipes in this book were made in Seattle, where we have higher humidity than most cities. If you're in a dryer climate, decrease flour by 2 tablespoons to ¼ cup total for cookie recipes. If you're at higher than 70% humidity, increase flour by 2 tablespoons to ¼ cup total for cookies.